The Little B<

Real Estate Definitions

Asia Pacific

Editor:

Peter Barge, F.A.P.I., F.C.I.A.

Contributors:

Takeshi Akagi, Zameer Bandukwalla, Christopher Brown, Dorothy Chow,
Dave Colverson, Annabelle Doublier, John Dunn, Ian Gordon, Richard Johnson,
Anna Kalifa, Graham Kennedy, Kwang Inn Kwa, Colin Moore, Jane Murray,
Rod Routh, Jeremy Smith, Benjawan Suewongprayoon, John Talbot,
Keng Chiam Tan, Harold Tan, James Tyrrell, Millie Wong, Jane Wu, Holly Yang.

The Little Book of
Real Estate Definitions
Asia Pacific

Jones Lang LaSalle

John Wiley & Sons (Asia) Pte. Ltd.

Copyright © 2006, Jones Lang LaSalle. All rights reserved.
Published by John Wiley & Sons (Asia) Pte. Ltd.
2 Clementi Loop, #02-01, Singapore 129809

No part of this publication may be reproduced, stored in a retrieval system, or transmitted in any form or by any means, electronic, mechanical, photocopying, recording, scanning, or otherwise, except as expressly permitted by law, without either the prior written permission of the Publisher, or authorization through payment of the appropriate photocopy fee to the Copyright Clearance Center. Requests for permission should be addressed to the Publisher, John Wiley & Sons (Asia) Pte. Ltd., 2 Clementi Loop, #02-01, Singapore 129809, tel: (65) 6463-2400, fax: (65) 6463-4605, e-mail: enquiry@wiley.com.sg.

This publication is designed to provide accurate and authoritative information with regard to the subject matter covered. It is sold with the understanding that the Publisher is not engaged in rendering professional services. If professional advice or other expert assistance is required, the services of a competent professional person should be sought.

Other Wiley Editorial Offices

John Wiley & Sons, Inc., 111 River Street, Hoboken, NJ 07030, USA
John Wiley & Sons Ltd., The Atrium, Southern Gate, Chichester PO19 BSQ, England
John Wiley & Sons (Canada) Ltd., 5353 Dundas Street West, Suite 400, Toronto, Ontario M9B 6H8, Canada
John Wiley & Sons Australia Ltd., 42 McDougall Street, Milton, Queensland 4064, Australia
Wiley-VCH, Boschstrasse 12, D-69469 Weinheim Germany

Library of Congress Cataloging-in-Publication Data:

ISBN - 13 978-0470-82211-1
ISBN - 10 0470-82211-2

Typeset in 10-14 point, Times by Superskill
Printed in Singapore by Saik Wah Press Pte. Ltd.
10 9 8 7 6 5 4 3 2 1

abandonment The act of voluntarily giving up a right (of ownership or lease or any other right) over a property.

absentee landlord / owner Owner of a property who resides elsewhere (usually in another city or country).

absolute title The right of ownership of a legal estate in registered land; a title that is guaranteed by the state that no one has a better title that is subject to any minor interests or overriding interests.

abstract Summary of a lengthy document or piece of writing which contains all or most of the salient points of the original.

abut Adjacent or contiguous to. For example, if a property is adjacent or next to another, it can be said to abut each other.

accelerated depreciation An accounting term indicating any method of depreciation which allows owners to claim depreciation benefits at rates greater than those calculated under the straight-line method.

acceleration clause This is a clause in a loan deed or mortgage agreement that allows the lender to demand full and immediate repayment of a loan. It is usually triggered by an event such as default in the payment of installments or a change in the ownership.

acceptance The act of voluntarily agreeing to accept an offer.

access right The right to enter and exit one's property from a public road or land or thoroughfare. This right is usually implied in all property transactions in almost all parts of the world, i.e., any transaction involving property is deemed to include the right to enter and exit that property. However, it is prudent to obtain legal advice on this matter as some less developed countries or jurisdictions may not guarantee this right or may require that a separate application be made to obtain right of access upon payment of certain fees to the local authority.

accessory buildings Annexes to a building such as servants' quarters, sheds, garages, etc.

accessory parcel (*MYS*) Any parcel shown in a strata plan, which is used in conjunction with a parcel.

accommodation value (AV) (*HKG*) A unit rate of site value or land price, obtained by dividing the site value or land price by the floor area of the proposed development on the site.

accord Agreement by which a creditor accepts less than the full consideration of the contract as full and final settlement of dues/ liabilities under that contract. An agreement to this effect between a creditor and debtor is known as "Accord and Satisfaction."

accounts payable Amounts owed to creditors for goods and services bought on credit.

accounts receivable Amounts due to a business from customers for goods and services sold on credit.

accrual method of accounting Method of accounting that recognizes revenue when earned and expenses when incurred in order to appropriately match income with expenses in an accounting period.

accrue To become due and to increase as a result thereof.

accrued expenses The obligation to pay business expenses that were incurred, but not paid, during an accounting period.

accrued interest The unpaid interest accumulated from an investment or a loan.

accumulated amortization A deduction from intangible assets to show the total amount of periodic charges to income over the estimated useful lives of those assets. Also called Reserve for Depreciation.

accumulated depreciation A deduction from fixed assets to show the total amount of periodic charges to income over the estimated useful lives of those assets. Also called Reserve for Depreciation.

accumulated interest Interest dues that have accumulated as a result of non-payment in the past.

accumulation index Financial index reflecting total return i.e., price appreciation and income return combined.

acquisition costs The cost of acquiring a property; includes purchase price and all other allied costs like insurance and legal fees, brokerage charges, etc.

acre An area of land of any shape containing 43,560 square feet or 4,840 square yards or approximately 4,047 square meters.

acre foot A volume of space covering one acre and with a depth of one foot (43,560 cubic feet or 1,233 cubic meters).

acreage Vacant land. Also refers to any plot of land that is measured in acres or any plot of land that has no sub-divisions.

act of god Damage caused by nature. Examples: floods, hurricanes, tsunamis, etc. Also known as *force majeure*. An unexpected event that prevents one from complying with certain terms and conditions in a contract.

action to quiet title Legal proceedings that conclusively establish ownership over a property.

actual cash value The price at which a property can be sold at a given point of time.

ad valorem Literally, according to the value. Applied, for instance, to a scale of stamp duty, inheritance tax or fees.

addendum Something that is added to an existing document. Example: supplementary to an agreement.

additions Modifications to a building by adding on structures or creation of additional space, resulting in an increase in dimensions or useable or covered areas.

ad-hoc Latin term signifying a decision for a given situation only or specific to.

adjacent Next to. May or may not be connected to.

adjoining Next to and connected to.

adjustable mortgage loans (AMLS) Also called floating rate loans, flexible rate loans, variable rate loans and adjustable rate loans. Here, the rate of interest varies and is adjusted from time to time to coincide with the rate prevailing in the economy or to a pre-determined peg.

adjusted gross income Total rental income of a property at full capacity minus amounts that cannot be collected on account of vacancies and other reasons.

administrator A person appointed by a court to manage an estate while testamentary proceedings are on. This person also distributes the estate of a deceased person in accordance with the orders of the court.

adverse gearing Where the total annual cost of borrowed money on a property or project exceeds the net rental income.

adverse possession (*HKG*) Possessory title to land which is gained by occupying the land for a specific period of time, without the interference of the land owner.

aerial survey A survey of an area made by taking sequential photographs from an aircraft; plans are then drawn from the photographs.

aesthetic value The value of a property deriving from its architectural beauty or natural or manmade surroundings.

affidavit A statement or declaration made in writing and under oath before a competent (usually court) official.

affirmation Substitute for an oath.

afforestation The planting of a forest where none previously existed.

agency Person or body corporate acting under the orders and authority of another. The scope of such authority is usually specified in the agreement between the two parties.

agency agreement (agency listing) The term describing a listing under which the broker's commission is protected against a sale by other agents and often by the principal.

agent One who acts on behalf of a principal.

agent's commission The fee payable for services rendered by a real estate professional.

agrarian Relating to land, or to a division or distribution of land.

agreement for lease/sale It is a contract by which land or property is leased or sold by one party to another.

agricultural property Land which is used for agricultural purposes or for the purpose of raising livestock.

air rights This is the right to use the space above a property. It does not include the right to use the land surface on which the property is located.

AJB (Akte Jual Beli) (*IDN*) Deed of release (of land title).

alienate land (*MYS*) To dispose of state land in perpetuity or for a term of years, in consideration of the payment of rent, otherwise in accordance with the provisions of Sections 76 of the National Land Code 1965.

alienation To transfer the ownership of a property from one person to another.

alley A narrow path.

allodial tenure Absolute right of ownership over real estate assets which can be bequeathed/sold/gifted or otherwise disposed of by the owner according to his wishes.

alterations Modifications in a building without changes to its dimensions.

alternative user value The value of land and buildings which reflects a prospective use which is different from that of the current use.

amendment A change or alteration in an agreement or court document.

amenities Those facilities, like swimming pools, jogging tracks, health clubs, etc., which add value to a building.

amortization 1) The concept of writing off the capital cost of a wasting physical asset by means of a sinking fund. 2) Payment of a debt in equal installments of principal and interest, as opposed to interest only payments.

amortization rate The rate of interest used for purposes of amortization. The percentage of a periodic payment that is applied to the reduction of the principal; in a level-payment mortgage this corresponds to the sinking fund factor.

amortization term The period, usually expressed as a number of years coinciding with the useful life of an asset, over which the value of the asset is written off.

amortize To bring down outstanding debt by regular payments referred to above.

anchor tenant One or more department or variety chain stores, supermarkets or hypermarkets, introduced into a shopping center in key positions to attract the shopping public into the center for the purpose of encouraging other retailers to lease shops en route. The larger the development the more anchors required.

ancillary use A planning term describing the use of a property in a manner different from, but functionally related to, its main use.

annexure A written or visual addendum which is attached to a legal document (not necessarily an agreement), e.g., floor plan, structural certificate, etc.

annual debt service Amounts of principal and debt repayments due per year.

annual sinking fund A sinking fund where payments and interest accumulated are calculated yearly.

annual value (AV) (*SGP*) AV is used as the basis to compute property tax for properties in Singapore. Currently, the rate of tax is 10%. AV is the gross annual rental value which a property is expected to fetch when let and less what the landlord pays for expenses of repair and maintenance.

annuity The payment of a certain sum of money to a person annually for life or for a given period of years.

annuity method Method for appraising the present value of a property which takes into account expected future incomes before depreciation.

API (*AUS*) Australian Property Institute (professional body).

apartment A form of property ownership in which each owner holds title to his/her individual unit, similar to western definition of condominium.

apartment hotel A property offering guests a complete self-contained sole occupancy unit consisting of bedrooms, a living room, a kitchen with full cooking facilities and dining area. Usually requires a hotel license to operate as such. Serviced apartments which are let on a daily basis function like an apartment hotel.

application list (*HKG*) List of government lands announced by the government, out of which developers may apply for the sale of the sites via public auction.

appraisal Alternative term for valuation.

appraiser One who carries out appraisals (valuations). The term is used in the USA for a valuer.

appreciation Increase in the value of a property.

arbitrage The system by which dealing in securities is carried out in order to profit from a variation in the price quoted in different markets. Often effected by buying and selling in two different markets at the same time in order to profit from the margin.

arbitration A method of resolving a disagreement between two parties by presenting their different views to an independent arbitrator. The award is binding on the parties but an arbitrator's decision can be challenged in a court of law under certain circumstances.

arbitration clause A clause in a contract providing for disputes arising from the contract to be referred for the decision of a third party (arbitrator). Common examples are disputes over rent review clauses in leases or the terms of building contracts.

arbitrator An impartial person who is appointed to settle a difference between two parties.

ar-karn (*THA*) Building.

ar-karn-chud (condominium) (*THA*) Strata-title building.

ar-karn-soong (*THA*) High-rise building with a height of 23 meters or more.

ar-karn-yai-pi-ses (*THA*) Extra large buildings that have gross floor area of 10,000 sq. m. or more.

arm's length Term implying the absence of any special relationship between two parties that could lead to claims of partiality or impropriety.

arrears 1) Money paid after the due date. Thus a debt is in "arrears" if unpaid after the due date. 2) Rent is said to be paid in arrears where the lease provides for the rent for a particular period to be paid at the end of that period.

ar-sang-ha-rim-ma-sup (*THA*) Real estate.

"as is" condition The sale, purchase, lease or conveyance of a property or item in its existing state, i.e., without any change, improvement, addition, alteration or repair. Also called "as is where is" in some countries.

asbestos A material that is resistant to fire and heat and was previously used in insulation. It is now linked to cancer.

asking price The price at which vendor offers a property for sale. The eventual selling price may be different after negotiation with the purchaser.

assess To calculate the value or worth of a property usually for the purpose of taxes or sale.

assessed value The value assigned to a property by a tax authority.

assessment The act of assessing.

assessment (*MYS*) A form of building tax, which is payable to the local authority. This tax is calculated as a percentage of annual value and varies with the property type.

asset Something owned by and having continuing value to its owner or a business.

asset allocation Allocation of a portfolio between real estate, equities, bonds and cash based on a fund manager's risk-return preferences.

asset management Active approach to asset acquisition / disposal and property management with the objective of optimizing asset performance.

asset valuation In the property market, this expression is applied to the valuation of land and buildings or plant and machinery. The term is often used to describe an expert opinion of the worth of a property which may be incorporated into company accounts, where the ownership of the asset is not necessarily to be transferred but the valuation is of interest to, for example, shareholders or is required for company takeovers, share flotations or mortgages.

assign Transfer any interest or the right of ownership over a property or any other asset.

assignee One who receives the right of ownership over a property or any other asset.

assignment The act of transferring ownership of something from one person to another.

assignment of lease The transfer by a lessee of all his rights over a leased property. In such a case, the assignee becomes a lessee under the original lessee. Some leases contain clauses specifying the conditions under which leases can be assigned. Assignment of lease is different from sub-lease and the two should not be used as synonyms.

assignor The person who assigns an agreement to another.

association dues Refers to charges for the Building and Common Area maintenance. This is also sometimes referred to as condominium dues.

assumption fee The fee charged by a lender for processing the paperwork required for transferring an existing loan to another person.

assumption of deed of trust Agreement by which a buyer agrees to take over the liabilities for the payment of an existing mortgage or deed of trust. The lender usually has to approve the buyer before such a transaction can go through.

atrium A large, centrally located hall in a building which is open all the way through to the roof, which is usually made of glass or other transparent material. This allows light to stream in.

attest To certify.

attic The space between the ceiling and roof of a structure.

auction A process of selling land or property by public bidding.

authority approvals The necessary sign-off by council, fire department, government, etc., confirming design compliance with laws to enable a facility to be constructed or a transaction to be completed.

average check Average check is the amount a single diner will spend on food and beverage, excluding tax and tip. It is often computed by dividing food and beverage revenue by the total number of diners served.

average daily rate (ADR) Room revenue divided by rooms sold.

average daily traffic Average number of vehicles or people using a thoroughfare over a certain period.

average length of stay The average length of stay in hotels is a statistical calculation often computed by dividing the total number of nights by the number of guests stayed; as in hospitals, the average length of stay is computed by the total number of days of care, counting the date of admission but not the date of discharge, by the number of patients discharged.

average rate Average price charged per unit of goods or services sold. It may refer to interest, prices of goods, units of utility consumption, etc. In taxation, where ad valorem taxes are levied at progressive rates, it is the average value of tax paid on the entire body of goods or income on which such taxes are levied.

average room rate (per occupied room) The average room rate in hotels is a statistical calculation often computed by dividing rooms revenue by the total number of guest rooms occupied.

aviation easement An easement over private property next to airport runways, which limits the height of crops, trees and structures in an aircraft's flight path.

award The amount paid for a property taken over by the state for a public purpose.

awning A sheet of cloth, canvas or metal which protrudes over a door or window and provides protection from the sun and the rain.

backfill To refill ground that had been dug up for construction or development purposes.

backup offer Secondary offer made to protect one's interests in case the first offer fails.

baffle An acoustic barrier often inserted above a ceiling to provide soundproofing.

bai-anu-yard-chai-arkarn (*THA*) Building permit.

bai-anu-yard-kor-sang (*THA*) Construction permit.

balance sheet A report showing the financial position or condition of a business at a given date. Also called Statement of Financial Position or Statement of Financial Condition.

balcony An area with a wall or bars around it that is joined to the outside wall of a building on an upper level.

balloon payment A repayment of a loan or bond, usually but not necessarily the final repayment, which is larger in amount than the preceding or earlier installments. This kind of arrangement is referred to as "ballooning" a loan.

bank guarantee (performance guarantee) A secured promissory note provided by a financial institution on behalf of a contractor or party as a guarantee of its performance often used in lieu of retention.

bankrupt A situation where the liabilities of a business or an individual are greater than the assets, making it impossible to meet debts and other outstandings.

bare shell Property that is delivered to buyer without decoration.

base rent The minimum rent for a commercial property without taking into account any add-ons like percentage of sales/profit that make up the total lease package.

base rent abatement During any period of reconstruction or repair after a major casualty, if the lessee's ability to conduct business in the demised premises is materially hindered or impaired, the base rent and any maintenance charges due from the lessee will abate during the period in which the demised premises is unusable.

base year The year which forms the base for all future calculations of rents or values.

basement An underground or partially underground level, below the ground floor of a building.

basis point One-hundredth of one percentage point.

beam Long, stout piece of wood, metal or concrete that sits atop two or more pillars or walls and supports the weight of the structure above.

bearer The holder of a commercial instrument.

bearer instruments Commercial instruments like bonds, checks, etc., that give the person having it (bearer) the right to encash it.

bedrock Solid rock below the earth.

bedroom community A residential area outside a central city area.

bench mark A standard against which other things are judged. Often used in surveys to determine the height or distance of a structure.

beneficial estate Estate or property the ownership or enjoyment of which will vest in the intended beneficiary after a period of time, usually in terms of a will or a trust deed.

beneficial interest An interest in property held by a beneficiary who is not necessarily the owner of the legal interest, e.g., where a legal estate is owned by a trustee (trustees) under a trust entitling the beneficiary to the financial rewards available after meeting all due obligations.

beneficial owner 1) A person enjoying or entitled to property for his own benefit, not, for instance, as a trustee who holds the legal estate in land for the benefit of another. The owner of the legal estate is usually the beneficial owner, but if the legal estate is vested in trustees, the beneficial owner has only an equitable interest. He is then known as the beneficiary or *cestui que trust*. 2) The person who is the real owner of a security, and thereby entitled to all consequential benefits, as distinct from a nominee who holds securities on behalf of another.

beneficiary Someone who receives property or offer assets in a will. Someone for whose benefit a trust is set up.

bequeath To give property by way of a will.

bequest Property that is given to someone by a will.

best rent The highest rent which can reasonably be expected by a landlord in the circumstances of a particular case.

betterment Any improvement to a property.

bid An offer to buy or construct or build something where more than one party is (usually) interested.

bill of quantities (BoQ) A schedule of all labor and material items required to construct a facility that is priced on an itemized basis.

bill of sale A document transferring property to another.

billboard A flat board affixed to land or buildings where advertisements are posted.

binding obligations The rights and duties agreed upon and described in an agreement executed between two parties that are binding upon the parties to the agreement (eg. landlord and tenant or vendor and purchaser).

BKPM (*IDN*) Investment Coordinating Board.

blighted area An area that is run-down and decrepit looking.

blind corner Corner where drivers cannot see traffic coming at right angles because of the presence of some visual obstruction.

block An area in a city enclosed by roads on all sides.

blue chip The description given to a corporation or company with a high level of financial stability, e.g., a government department or large corporation.

board resolution A legally binding document executed by the board member of the corporate which authorizes certain acts or decisions to be carried out by the company. A board resolution can form part of the agreement and may be required by the lessor and the lessee before the agreement is executed.

bojeungbu walsei (hybrid structure) (*KOR*) A rental system that incorporates a blend of the chonsei and walsei rental structure. Includes a higher than normal security deposit (less than chonsei, however) and a lower monthly rent than a walsei rent. Service charge is still due on a monthly basis.

bojeunggum (lease key money) (*KOR*) Security deposit. Under the lease, a bojeunggum is payable upon signing the lease and normally equivalent to 10 times the monthly rental amount in the case of walsei rental structure. This amount shall be deposited without any interest rate during the lease term and can be increased during rental reviews throughout the term of the lease, but the total amount is returned to the tenant at the expiration of the lease.

bona fide Legal term meaning actions, or individuals that are honest and in good faith.

bond A deed by which one agrees to indemnify another person against losses suffered on account of acts of omission or commission by the former. Also means a debt security.

boodongsan (*KOR*) Real estate.

booga gachi-se (value-added tax) (*KOR*) VAT at the rate of 10% is applied to the supply of goods and services by a taxable entity. "Goods" includes the supply of buildings and "services" includes the supply of the contractual or legal right to use the goods.

book depreciation Depreciation shown in the books of accounts.

book gain/loss A notional gain or loss represented by the difference between acquisition cost of an asset, as shown in the accounts, and its market value at a particular time.

book value The value which is ascribed to a property shown in the accounts as a capital asset but is not necessarily current market value, since it may be based on actual cost (less depreciation, if any) or on an earlier valuation after acquisition.

boonyang (*KOR*) Sales for strata title.

boulevard Wide, tree-lined street.

boundary The line or structure separating two contiguous properties, states or countries.

boundary mark (*MYS*) Any survey stone, iron pipe, or spike, wooden peg or post, concrete post or pillar or other mark used for the purpose of making boundaries.

BPHTB (*IDN*) Transfer tax which is payable for any real estate transaction.

BPN (Badan Pertanahan Nasional) (*IDN*) National Land Agency.

breach of contract An act or omission, contrary to one or more provisions in a contract and therefore giving the aggrieved party a right to enforce specific performance, to rescind the contract and/or to claim damages, the remedy available depending upon the nature of the breach.

breach of covenant Failure to adhere to the terms of a promise.

breach of warranty Failure to comply with a contractual undertaking, e.g., the failure of a vendor to pass title or give vacant possession when such has been warranted. Such a breach normally entitles the innocent party to damages, although the breach of a warranty in an insurance contract by the insured normally entitles the insurer to treat the contract as discharged.

break clause A clause in the lease which gives the landlord and/or the tenant a right, in specified circumstances, to terminate the lease before its normal expiry date. It usually defines the length of the notice to be given and may be subject to contractual or statutory financial provisions.

break-even point A financial state where total income is the same as total expenditure, leaving no profit or loss.

break-even analysis A cash flow technique, which, on such assumptions as are made, shows the profit (or loss) of a project and its break-even point.

break-up value The value of a specific property, e.g., an estate of land and building, based on the assumption that it is lotted and sold in parts, in such a manner as to achieve the best possible price.

bridge A road or a pathway built over a river, gorge or other natural or manmade obstruction to allow the passage of vehicular or human traffic to the opposite side.

bridge financing A loan which is generally given to allow the borrower to tide over some immediate requirement while he awaits a more permanent or long-term solution to his financial needs.

brief A document that identifies the clients' needs and requirements that will be developed into a design for the contractor to construct.

British thermal unit (BTU) Unit of heat used to describe the capacity of heating and cooling systems.

broker/dealer A person who brings together a buyer and a seller in return for a commission (usually a percentage of the total deal value).

brokerage 1) Commission paid to a broker. 2) The activity of a broker in bringing together two parties in a transaction.

brokerage commission The amount paid as consideration to a broker.

buffer strip (buffer zone) Portion or strip of land between two areas.

build to suit A property custom built to suit the specifications of the long-term lessee.

builder One who builds buildings.

builder bond A bond issued by a builder to ensure the completion of a building (see bank guarantee).

building A manmade structure where people live, meet or carry out business. Example: house, office, mall, temple, etc.

building application (BA) An application to the local authority relating to the detailed design and construction of a proposed building.

building code A list of laws, conventions and practices that govern the construction and maintenance of real estate assets.

Building Code of Australia (BCA) (*AUS*) sets minimal building standards.

building completion date The date provided by the landlord by which date the building is made operational in all aspects including all onsite and offsite works (described in detail in the agreement), obtaining the necessary approvals including Occupation Certificate, for the demised premises to be occupied.

building consent Authority approval for building work.

Building Construction Authority (BCA) (*SGP*) The primary role of BCA is to develop and regulate Singapore's building and construction industry. BCA issues the TOPs and CSCs, approve structural plans and permit building works.

building contract A contract between an owner or occupier of land and a building contractor, setting forth the terms under which construction is to be undertaken. A contract will normally include details of work to be carried out, basis of remuneration, time-scale, and penalties, if any, for failure to comply with terms of the contract.

building contractor A builder who enters into a contract under which he becomes obligated to carry out building or engineering works of a nature, extent and specification described in the contract and usually within a prescribed period.

building insurance replacement cost The estimated construction costs of a replacement building. It is to be covered by the insurance policy against losses due to structural damage caused by fire only and does not include any consequential loss and liabilities to third parties.

building line The line on a street or area beyond which no construction can take place. Its purpose is to ensure that buildings are not built too close to each other or to the street.

building permit A permit granted by the construction or building authority to construct a building.

Building Plan approval (BP) (*SGP*) This refers to the approval granted by the Commissioner of Building Control in respect of building plans and specifications submitted in accordance with the prescribed building regulations in force. BP approval is needed before construction can begin and before a sales license can be granted.

building residual technique A method of disaggregating the value of land from the total value of a property to arrive at the value of the building.

building restrictions Restraints placed on the absolute right of a property owner from building whatever he wants.

building warrant of fitness (*NZL*) An annual certificate signed by the building owner or manager saying that requirements under the compliance schedule for the property have been met.

built-ins Utilitarian items like cupboards, bathtubs, stoves, ovens, etc., that are built into the building so as to make them immovable.

bullet A borrowing in which the repayment of the entire principal is made at maturity.

business park An integrated development whereby businesses are provided with common infrastructure, facilities and services. This results in lower costs and, therefore, greater competitiveness for individual businesses.

business tax (营业税) (*CHN*) Business tax is levied at 5% on gross rental income for property leases and 5% on total sales value for property sales.

buttress Something that provides support to a wall.

buyer's market In the property market, a condition of supply and demand in which those seeking to purchase are in a relatively strong negotiating position because of a degree of oversupply.

by-laws Internal rules that govern the activities of a company, association or society.

call A demand for repayment of a loan. In India and some other countries, it also refers to an informal short-term inter-corporate loan market, where money is lent and borrowed by large companies based on verbal agreements between the parties.

call date Date on which a call (loan) is due.

call option A contract whereby one party has the option to purchase the other party's interest in a property, usually within a specified time, at a stated or calculable price and/or in defined circumstances. It is binding against a third party only if registered as an estate contract.

cancellation clause Clause in an agreement that sets out the conditions under which, and the terms on which, the contract can be cancelled or terminated.

cap The upper limit of something. Example: a cap of 7 per cent in a floating rate interest agreement means the maximum interest charged cannot exceed 7 per cent.

capita Heads. Usually used in conjunction with the prefix "per." Per capita means per head.

capital Wealth usually derived from direct or indirect savings, in the form of permanent or durable assets or employed in industrial, commercial or other productive enterprises as the financial base upon which they are established and operate. This is with a view to making a profit, which may be either income or a capital gain, or both. Typically, it is the money invested by the purchase of stocks and shares in a corporate body, the aggregate of which represents the capital of that company. In taxation, distinction between capital and income has to be drawn, as different rates of tax often apply to each.

capital asset pricing model (CAPM) Quantitative model explaining asset returns based on the relative risk of associated returns and the risk-free rate.

capital assets Permanent assets the benefits of which are expected to be enjoyed beyond the financial year in which they were purchased, e.g., trucks bought by a transport company are capital assets for the buyer but for the automobile company that makes and sells them, they are stocks or inventory.

capital expenditures Money spent on assets the benefit of which is expected to be enjoyed well beyond the financial year in which such expenditure is incurred. Example: expenditure incurred on buying plant and machinery, land and buildings, etc.

capital flow Movement of funds between different property markets/ sectors.

capital gains Profits earned from the sale of capital assets.

capital gains tax A tax payable on capital gains resulting from property and other investments.

capital improvement Work carried out on an asset with a view to enhancing its value, but not including repairs or maintenance.

capital markets Markets which deal in financial products such as stocks, bonds, etc.

capital value The overall value of a property as distinct from its annual periodic return. Capital value may be established in a number of different ways. In the simplest case it is calculated by multiplying the annual return (net rent) by the inverse of the yield.

capitalization The estimation of a property's value on the basis of its earning capacity.

capitalization approach Refers to a method of computing the capital value of a property by multiplying its net annual income by the inverse of the capitalization rate. Also known as the investment method of valuation.

capitalization rate The yield at which the net income from an investment is discounted to ascertain its capital value at a given date.

capitalization ratio The relationship that each security (debt or equity) bears to total debt and equity, less intangible assets, expressed as a ratio.

capitalized value The present value of a property as determined by capitalizing its future estimated income.

carpet area Carpet area of a property is defined as the net usable area, from the inner sides of one wall to another. The expression "carpet area" shall mean and comprise of the following: the carpet area of the demised premise, toilet areas within the demised premises, AHU room/s within the demised premises and dedicated service areas for the demised premises.

carrying charges The cost of maintaining an income-producing property during periods when it is not doing so, e.g., maintenance costs of a new house that has not yet been leased, or the cost of maintaining a house between two leases.

case law Judicial interpretation of statutes in areas not specifically covered by any laws or judgments that interpret laws in a manner not originally intended by the framers of that law. The judgments, thus, create precedents which form the basis of future interpretations.

cash accounting A system of accounting which takes into account incomes and expenditures only when money exchanges hands and not when they are transacted.

cash back A payment made by a property owner to a prospective tenant to secure a letting in times of oversupply on terms which would otherwise be unacceptable. In essence it can be regarded as the opposite of a premium and, as such, is a form of reverse or negative premium.

cash flows The actual or estimated movement of money by way of income and outgoings during the life of a project.

cash flows analysis/statement Cash flow portrayed as a table of successive periods, e.g., monthly, quarterly or yearly. It has many applications relating to financial viability, e.g., forecasting loss, breakeven or profit; discounted cash flow exercises; or as a basis for budget control.

cashier's check (cheque) A check where a bank draws a check upon itself instead of its depositor's account. The depositor, who instructs the bank to do so and provides the money for it, does not have the right to stop payment. Buyers often insist on this mode of payment while closing sales. Also called a Banker's Draft, Bank Check or Demand Draft in some countries.

casino A licensed public room or building for gambling and other entertainment.

catchment area Area served by a commercial property such as a mall or market, or an area serviced by a school or a hospital. Also means the area drained by a river.

causeway Raised road usually across low lying lands.

caveat (*SGP*) A document which any person who claims to have an interest in the property may lodge against the title of property at the Registry of Land Titles.

caveat emptor Latin for buyers beware. Legal term meaning the quality risk in a transaction vests with the buyer, unless specifically stated otherwise or unless fraud or deception can be proved. Most countries, however, now have strict laws protecting buyers from shoddy workmanship, finish and quality.

cavity wall Two brick walls joined at the top and hollow inside.

cc&r's (covenants, conditions and restrictions) Limits and restrictions placed on properties.

central business district (CBD) The functional center around which the rest of a city is structured. Characterized by the presence of comparison shopping, office accommodation, leisure facilities, buildings for recreational use, public museums, art galleries and governmental functions.

central city Main city of a cluster of cities. Also means the downtown area of a city.

Central Provident Fund (CPF) (*SGP*) The CPF is a comprehensive social security savings plan which has provided many working

Singaporeans with a sense of security and confidence in their old age. CPF is contributed by both the employee and employer and can be used for purchase of properties, investments as well as healthcare, although the actual withdrawal of CPF can only be done at age 55.

Central Provident Fund Board (*SGP*) A statutory board in charge of the administration of CPF. It also sets the percentage of distribution to the various accounts as well as the percentage contribution from employees and employers.

certificate of compliance (滿意紙) (*HKG*) A certificate issued to the registered owner of property when the Director of Lands is satisfied that all the positive obligations imposed by the general and special conditions in the land lease governing the lot have been complied with.

certificate of deposit (CD) A document issued by a bank or other institution certifying that a person has deposited a certain sum of money with it for a specified period of time. The depositor is paid a fixed or floating rate of interest, but cannot withdraw any sum of money before the maturity date without paying a penalty (usually in form of forfeiting part of the interest promised).

certificate of occupancy Certificate issued by a local authority stating that a building is fit for occupation.

certificate of practical completion Under a building contract, a certificate issued by the architect, surveyor or supervising officer stating that the works have been substantially completed and the building is ready for occupation. This certificate will: a) release an agreed percentage of any retention money; b) begin the defects liability period; and c) transfer responsibility for insurance from the contractor to the employer.

certificate of purchase Certificate issued to a buyer, usually following a court-ordered sale, stating that he has purchased a certain property. The buyer will be entitled to transfer the title to the property to his own name if the original owner does not redeem the property within a specified date.

Certificate of Statutory Completion (CSC) (*SGP*) A certificate issued by the building authority to certify that all building works have been completed in accordance with regulations.

certificate of title (*NZL*) A document attesting to the rights of ownership to a piece of land describing the land involved, the area, the legal description, the type of ownership and any listed mortgages, charges, leases, easements and other encumbrances.

certified check A personal check which a bank guarantees to pay. The bank usually ensures that the issuer has enough funds in his account to honor the check and does not clear other checks if they deplete the funds in the issuer's account to the point where there's not enough money to cover the amount of the certified check. Banks also do not honor stop payments on certified checks.

certified copy A document that is certified by a competent authority to be a true copy of its original.

chaebol (*KOR*) A large business conglomerate.

chae-kwon (*KOR*) Bond.

chain of title The chronological list of owners of a property since the earliest records to the present times.

chain store Several stores belonging to the same owner, having similar layout design and other features which point to a central authority and which distinguishes them from others.

channel A passageway for the passage of wiring, sewage, water or gas. A channel may be open or covered, on the ground or underground. Also means a long, open-ended depression through which water flows.

charge Acts as an encumbrance on title and involves no transfer of title to, or of possession of, the property as security for the loan. The property is designated as that which can be taken in execution of the debt on default.

chattel A property other than an interest in land. Property, other than real estate, owned by an individual. Also called personal property.

chia (甲) (**TWN**) It is a traditional measurement unit of area used in Taiwan. Its use is limited to real estate. 1 chia = 0.96992 hectare = 2.3968 acre.

Chinese wall A term used, particularly in relation to the world of business and finance, to describe an intangible barrier existing within an organization to prevent the improper flow and subsequent use of information from someone who is on one side of the barrier to anyone. The type of information not allowed to cross the barrier is that which, if disclosed, would be a breach of confidentiality and prejudicial to one or more clients of the organization or to anyone else to whom duty is owed. Such improper disclosure can only be prevented if the operational system adopted by an organization is efficient, understood by all to whom it applies, and imposes adequate penalties if breached.

chonsei (structure) (**KOR**) Traditional Korean rental method that involves depositing a large upfront amount (approximately 60-70% of the purchase value) and leasing the space without paying any monthly rent. Service charges are due monthly.

chonsei-kwon (**KOR**) A chonsei right is very similar to a kun-mortgage. Like the mortgage, the chonsei right comes into effect upon registration. However, unlike a mortgage, in the event that title to the premises is transferred to a third party, the chonsei right holder can continue to occupy and use the premises for the remainder of the existing term, except as against a party taking title in connection with foreclosure proceedings involving mortgagee claims that have priority over the chonsei right holder. In the event that the landlord fails to refund the key money deposit, the chonsei right holder may enjoy many of the rights enjoyed by a mortgagee, i.e., the right to foreclose upon the premises, etc. The time and procedures required for the foreclosure proceedings are also similar to that required for foreclosing against a mortgage. One significant difference is that the registration of a chonsei right may only be made with respect to a key money lease arrangement. Another difference is that a chonsei registration must be renewed every time the lease term is renewed.

city Large urban settlement with modern amenities.

city maintenance and construction tax（城市维护建设税）(*CHN*)　It is levied at 1-7% of business tax, depending on location and local government.

civil action　Legal action for remedy against some wrong that is not criminal in nature.

civil law　All laws other than laws dealing with crimes.

claim　Demand for some action or right.

class action　Legal action brought by a group of people who have similar claims against a common party.

claw-back　A lawful recovery of part or the whole of a payment which was properly due at the time it was made. The term is specifically used in relation to tax — originally as "the clawing back" by a taxpayer of some element of tax paid by him which proved to be excessive or on other grounds recoverable; more recently it tends to be a "clawing back" by the tax authority of some element of payment previously made to a taxpayer by way of tax relief.

clear title　Unencumbered title to real property, against which there are no claims, mortgages, voluntary liens, etc.

clearing house　A place where, at agreed dates, transactions of a commercial nature are settled by financial payments which equal the net result of any transactions carried out by parties concerned since the last date. In particular, that part of a financial market for commodities, securities or other assets which arranges for settlements of transactions at regular intervals.

cluster housing (*SGP*)　Cluster housing is a hybrid development which combines conventional housing with the features of condominium housing with strata titles, shared facilities such as swimming pools, landscaped gardens and other amenities but within a low-rise building form usually not exceeding four storeys in height.

cockloft (*HKG*)　An upper loft, a garret or the highest room in a building.

code of compliance certificate (*NZL*)　Certificate issued when building work is completed confirming that the construction complies with the New Zealand Building Code.

collateral (security) Traditionally used to mean some security in addition to the personal obligation of the borrower but commonly used to refer to a security provided in addition to the principal one.

collective (en-bloc) sales (*SGP*) An arrangement whereby owners of separate units of a private residential project or even commercial building pool their interests together and sell them collectively to a developer.

commercial mortgage backed security (CMBS) Security issued on a portfolio of loans, each of which is secured by commercial property.

commercial property Property that is used for business purposes only.

commingling The mixing of different kinds of funds. For example, if a company mixes funds it has collected as fixed deposits (which should be accounted for separately) with money collected as advance from buyers, it is known as commingling.

commission The payment of a percentage of the deal value as compensation to a broker for services rendered.

commitment 1) Title insurance term for the preliminary report issued before the actual policy. Said report shows the condition of title and the steps necessary to complete the transfer of title as contemplated by the buyer and seller. 2) A written promise to make or insure a loan for a specified amount and on specified terms.

common area The space within a shopping center or other estate or campus-type development which is not intended to be let. It may include landscaped areas, pedestrian precincts and service facilities.

common property (*SGP*) Any premises not included in the strata lot but within the strata-titled development. Examples of common property would include communal facilities like swimming pool and clubhouses as well as areas like lift lobbies and staircases.

common wall Wall separating two properties owned by different people.

community property Property owned jointly by a husband and wife. Also, in some countries, certain properties like forests, etc., owned collectively by the local, indigenous residents where individual members of that community have the right to use that property but no right of individual ownership or sale. The transfer of such properties to outsiders is not allowed.

community shopping center Mid-sized shopping center.

co-mortgagor When more than one person sign a mortgage, they are said to be co-mortgagors. Also means the person who guarantees the repayment of the amounts due, who signs the mortgage deed along with the person receiving the money.

comparables Similar properties to which a property can be compared in order to determine its value.

compensation Payment made for damages. Money paid by the government following the acquisition of land.

completion The final step in the legal process of transferring ownership of property, e.g., when the documents in connection with a sale of land are signed, sealed and delivered.

completion certificate/statement Certificate from a local authority stating that a building under construction is ready and complete.

compliance schedule (*NZL*) A local council document listing the inspection, maintenance and reporting procedures for safety systems such as fire alarms and lifts to ensure they are safe to use.

compulsory acquisition (*SGP*) Governed by the Land Acquisition Act, the State may acquire land for public interest or benefit.

compound interest Interest that is paid on the principal as well as on the interest that accumulates over time.

compulsory purchase The acquisition, in accordance with statutory procedures and practice, of interests in land by a public or private body empowered so to do by an Act and authorized to do so by the appropriate minister's or government entity's confirming a compulsory purchase order. Such a purchase entitles the purchaser to deprive the, usually unwilling, owner of his property on payment of such compensation as is provided for by statute.

computer listing A listing (of real estate, among other things) done on the internet that allows any user to zero in on their requirements (area of apartment, number of rooms, etc.).

concealed heating Heating system which passes hot air, steam or hot water through a network of pipes or coils concealed in walls, ceilings or floors.

Concept Plan (*SGP*) The Concept Plan is the long-term plan for Singapore's physical development for the next 40-50 years. The Concept Plan lays the foundation for the drafting of the Master Plan and was completed with extensive inputs from the public. It is revised every 10 years.

concession Permission granted by the owner of land or property to another party to use the said land or building for some business, in return for some monetary consideration.

condition precedent A condition to be performed before an agreement becomes effective or some right vests or accrues.

conditional sale of real property Land sale where the consideration amount is paid in installments. The title vests with the seller until the full amount is paid. The buyer has only equitable title until he pays the agreed amount in full.

conditional sales contract Sale of real estate where the title remains with the seller until the buyer fulfills certain conditions.

condominium A grouping of apartment blocks or other buildings with several dwelling units, usually with a range of shared facilities such as swimming pools, tennis courts, health club and landscaped gardens, etc. Each unit is owned by a different person; and the common areas are jointly owned by all such individual owners.

condominium map (plan) Map showing the common and private areas in a condominium.

condominium owners' association A body formed by the owners of individual dwelling units in a condominium that looks after and maintains the common services essential for the use of the condominium. It also represents the common interests of individual dwelling unit owners with outsiders.

conduction The transmission of electricity or heat.

conduit Channel through which something else passes.

confidentiality agreement (CA) (*AUS*) This is a common document used by vendors prior to releasing confidential information to prospective purchasers. It often carries the full weight of the law if breached.

Confirmed List (Government Land Sales Program) (*SGP*) Under the Government Land Sales program, sites which appear on the Confirmed List would be put up for sale by tender as scheduled.

conservation houses (*SGP*) Conserved buildings are selected by the Urban Redevelopment Authority based on their historical and architectural significance, rarity in terms of building types, styles and their contribution to the overall environment. There are also certain guidelines which restricts the use and additions and alterations (A&A) works that can be done on the conserved building.

consideration Strictly the payment, promise, object, or forbearance given by one party to a contract in return for a promise or pledge given by the other party. In property law, the term is applied particularly to the price offered by the purchaser in a contract to acquire an interest in land.

consolidation The merger of two or more properties into one.

construction cost The total cost of building a structure or house.

construction loan Loan taken to finance the cost of construction.

construction management Where a contractor is engaged to manage the construction of a project for an agreed fee and the trade contractors are engaged either directly by the client or on an open book basis.

construction period The length of time elapsing from the date a building or other similar project is started, or deemed to start, until the works involved are finished. The finishing date is frequently known as the date of practical completion, being the date when the architect certifies that all the relevant works have been carried out in a satisfactory manner.

consultant A company or individual who provides specialist advice and or services (typically architect, engineer, project manager).

consumer price index   Official indicator of price index of items used by a person in his daily life.

contemporary architecture   Modern architectural design.

contiguous   Bordering on.

contingency   Something that depends on something else to happen.

contingent fees   Fees that are paid only if some event takes place in future.

contract   Legally binding agreement.

contract for sale   1) Of land: An agreement whereby the seller (vendor) agrees to transfer an interest in land to a purchaser for a consideration. The agreement is effected by the exchange of copies of the agreement document between the parties. Rights to possession are not conferred upon the purchaser until the purchase is completed, but the purchaser has an insurable interest in the property from exchange of contracts. A non-returnable deposit is usually paid by the purchaser on exchange. 2) Of goods: The transfer of ownership of chattels from a seller to a buyer for a money price where ownership is transferred immediately.

contract rent   The amount of rent stipulated in the lease contract.

contraction rights   A collective name for any clause in a lease allowing a tenant to reduce in size either temporarily or permanently (eg., sub-lease, surrender, etc.).

contractor   One who undertakes to build a building or other structure in return for a fee.

contractor's method (*HKG*)   Valuation by aggregating the estimated land value and the estimated construction costs of a replacement building. This method is used for specialized or nonprofit making properties where there is no market.

contractor's overhead   Overhead expenses like cost of office, interest costs, etc., that a contractor has to incur.

contractor's profit   Selling price of a property minus input costs like land, labor materials, interest on loans and overheads.

convertible securities A debt or equity security that may under certain circumstances be exchanged for or converted into another security, generally common stock.

convex Curved outward.

convey To transfer title.

conveyance The act of transferring title.

conveyance tax Tax levied by the (usually local or state) government on the value of a property sale.

conveyancing The legal procedures employed in the creation, transfer and extinguishment of ownership of interests in land, including preparation of contracts, enquiries, searches, land registration (where appropriate) and completion of the transaction.

cooperative apartment A form of apartment ownership where the property itself is not sold; only shares in the company which owes the apartment are sold; one share entitles the owner to an apartment. Not very popular in many countries as financing is difficult to obtain in the absence of clear cut apartment ownership.

corner lot A property located at the crossing of two streets and having a frontage on both.

corporate real estate (CRE) Concerned with property related infrastructure which is integral to the running of a business.

corporation A corporate body that is set up for the purpose of running a business.

corridor A long passage in a building usually with rooms on either side.

co-signatory Someone, usually the guarantor, who signs a mortgage deed along with the person taking a loan. The liability for the loan falls upon the co-signatory in case the loanee defaults.

cost of living index An index that tracks the living expenses of an average person.

cost report A regular report that monitors the commitment and expenditure against the budget and may forecast the anticipated final cost.

cost-benefit analysis A method or technique to assist in decision-making, involving the consideration and measurement in financial terms of all costs and benefits, including social aspects, when comparing alternative projects or courses of action.

cost-of-living clause A clause in a contract, e.g. a lease providing for adjustment in price, rent or other financial item based upon an index such as the Retail Price Index.

cost-plus contract A building contract where the price is based upon the estimated or actual cost of the works together with (i.e., "plus") a proportion or agreed amount to represent the contractor's profit.

co-tenancy Tenancy taken on by two or more parties.

co-trustee Joint trustee.

counselor Lawyer.

counter offer A rival offer made in response to an initial offer.

county Administrative division within a country.

courtyard (四合院) (*CHN*) English term used for "siheyuan." The siheyuan is a traditional architectural style in Chinese culture. A siheyuan consists of a square housing compound, with rooms enclosing a central courtyard. In China, traditional courtyard housing is often one-storey.

covenant Any agreement whether written or implied between two parties.

covenant of quiet enjoyment Clause in a lease which guarantees peaceful possession to a tenant.

covenants running with the land Easements that pass with the title to the land.

creative financing Innovative financing options in lending.

credit The act by a bank of transferring money into a customer's account. It is also an accounting term for funds that have or will be received.

credit report A report on the past history of a person or company in meeting his debt repayment obligations.

critical path analysis A management technique (especially in project management) whereby a project is analyzed, and its activities and events (an activity taking place between two events) are portrayed as a network. The network may be used to demonstrate the project's duration.

cross lease (*NZL*) When each owner has an equal undivided share of the land but leases their own site and building from all the land owners.

cross section Graphic representation of a section formed by a plane that cuts an object, usually at right angles to its axis.

cross-easements Mutual easements annexed to two adjoining tenements, e.g., mutual rights of support between two contiguous buildings in different ownership.

cubic content The total volume in cubic feet of a building.

cubic foot The total volume enclosed by a cube that is 1 foot long x 1 foot wide x 1 foot deep. 35.3 cubic feet is equivalent to one cubic meter. A metric unit of volume, commonly used in expressing concentrations of a chemical in a volume of air.

cubic yard The total volume enclosed by a cube that is 1 yard long x 1 yard wide x 1 yard deep. 1.3 cubic yard equals one cubic meter.

cul de sac A street that is open at one end only.

culvert Drainage ditch which passes under a ramp or road.

curable depreciation Building repairs which are necessary for maintaining the value of a property but which haven't been made.

curb line The line separating the sidewalk or footpath from the road. Also called kerb line.

current assessed land value (公告現值) (*TWN*) A land value used by municipalities to compute land value increment tax; it is assessed once every year by municipalities. The value is close to the market value.

current assets Accounting term for cash-in-hand, checks in clearance, short-term debtors and other assets which are easily encashable.

current cost accounting A method of preparing a company's accounts in which the fixed assets are stated at their value to the business having regard to current rather than historic costs. The net current replacement cost is generally used, i.e., the present cost of acquiring a replacement asset that will provide the same service and output.

current liabilities Short-term debts.

current ratio The relationship of current assets to current liabilities, expressed as a ratio.

current yield The actual annual returns in percentage terms from an investment. For example, if a bond with a market value of $1,000 gives an annual return of $75, its current yield is 7.5 per cent.

curtain wall Exterior wall which lends no structural support to a building, but acts merely to enclose.

curtilege (*AUS*) The area of land around improvements required for the effective operation of those improvements e.g. access ways, driveways, gardens, etc.

cut-off date 1) The date on which an agreement or clause in an agreement ceases to have effect. 2) The last day of a period for calculating a certain payment or cost relating to an agreement.

daeriin (*KOR*) Attorney in law.

damages Money that courts order parties to pay as compensation for some loss they have caused to others. Also means a decline in the quality of material due to breakage, leakage, etc.

datum Reference point against which positions are plotted or measured.

datum line Line used to measure height.

dead load Weight of a truck or building, including all permanently affixed structure or appliances but not including the weight of things that are placed on or in it.

dead-end street Road or street that ends abruptly at a permanent obstacle. Street where the entry and exit point is the same.

debenture Written acknowledgement or evidence of a debt, especially stock issued as security by a company for borrowed money.

debt Money that is owed by one party to another.

debt amortization The practice of adjusting the original cost of a debt instrument as principal payments are received and any purchase discount or premium is written off to income over the life of the instrument.

debt service The regular and periodic payment of installments towards repayment of a loan.

decentralization The movement of people or transfer of power from a central position or authority to the suburbs or to subsidiary authorities.

decibel A measure of the loudness of sound.

declining balance method of depreciation Also known as the written down value or WD method of depreciation. In this, a fixed percentage of the residual value of an asset is written off every year.

decorate The act of adding to the beauty of a structure by making superficial changes.

decree An order of court.

dedicated The gift of private property for public use. Also means structure or equipment that is used for a single purpose only.

deed Legal document, usually pertaining to the ownership of a property.

deed of mutual covenant (DMC) (公契) (*HKG*) A contract entered into by the developer of the land, the building manager and the first party to purchase a unit in the development. The DMC sets out the details for the management and regulation of the multi-storey building and the details of the distribution of equal and undivided shares in the land.

deed of trust Document recording the terms of a trust.

default The failure to do something as required by law or failure to comply with certain terms and conditions in a contract. E.g., a "judgment in default" in favor of one party, where the other fails to comply with the required legal procedure. For instance, one party may default by not attending a court hearing or not serving a particular notice or counter notice.

defective title Title that is flawed.

defects liability period A specified term (normally 12 months) following practical completion of a facility when the contractor remains responsible to rectify any defective work.

deferred maintenance Repairs that are required to restore a property to good condition.

Deferred Payment Scheme (DPS) (*SGP*) This is a flexible payment scheme subject to limits imposed by the Controller of Housing. It requires the purchaser to exercise his option by signing the Sale & Purchase Agreement within three weeks of booking a unit and paying 5% of the purchase price as the booking fee. The remaining 5% (or 15%, depending on the loan quantum) of the downpayment is payable by the purchaser within eight weeks from the date of the Option. The rest of the purchase price may be deferred upon obtaining TOP or any time before that.

delay An occurrence that impacts on the time to complete an activity or the project.

delivery The act of handing over physical possession of a property to a buyer.

demand 1) A communication from a lender seeking payment of money owed to them. Various meanings in real estate, including level of leasing activity. 2) Level of interest in investment assets.

Demarcation District (DD) (*HKG*) During the period 1898 to 1904, a survey was carried out in the New Territories using relatively simple methods. This survey resulted in the production of about 600 map sheets known as Demarcation District (DD) sheets. These sheets show individual lot boundaries but without any grid reference to facilitate locating them on the ground. The plans were prepared at a scale of 16 inches or 32 inches to the mile (i.e., 1/3960 or 1/1980 respectively). Boundaries are shown graphically without any dimension and the accuracy of these sheets was relatively low. Lot areas were scaled off the DD sheets and the smallest unit of 0.01 acre was adopted for recording purposes.

demise Old expression for a life-long lease.

demised premises Defined in the agreement as the actual area being taken on lease or license or outright purchase.

demographics Statistics relating to population.

density In town planning, a term applied to the number of units permitted per acre (or hectare), usually in relation to residential accommodation.

department store Usually a multi-level retail property varying in size from one selling an extensive, but not comprehensive, variety of goods in at least 6,500 m² (70,000 sq. ft.) gross floor space to one selling a full range of different lines requiring about 23,000 m² (250,000 sq. ft.) of gross floor space. A distinctive feature of a department store is that it stocks a significant amount of clothing and household goods.

depletion Reduction in the value of a property.

deposit Money, often a token or smaller percentage of total price, that is paid to seal an agreement, pending the payment of a larger sum of money.

deposited plan (*NZL*) A survey plan giving legal definition to property boundaries.

depreciation Periodic charges to income to recognize the cost of "wear and tear" of a company's fixed assets over the estimated useful lives of those assets.

design & construct (D&C) contract An agreement with a party to provide the design and construction necessary to create a facility for a fee based on a detailed brief.

desk valuation A term indicating a valuation of a property by someone who has not made a physical inspection of a property for that purpose. Many believe that no property can be valued unless it has been physically inspected at the time of valuation.

detached houses/bungalow (*SGP*) A type of landed housing where by it comprises a detached dwelling house, usually not more than three storeys. The minimum plot size is 400 sq. m. and the frontage is 10 m.

deunggi (*KOR*) Official registration by the government.

developer An entrepreneur who has an interest in a property, initiates its development and ensures that this is carried out (for occupation, investment or dealing) and from the outset accepts the ultimate responsibility for providing or procuring the funds needed to finance the whole project.

developer's profit (or loss) The amount by which, on completion or partial completion of a development, the estimated value or the price realized on sale of a developer's interest exceeds (or is less than) the total outlay, including such figure for the land as is considered appropriate in the circumstances (including accrued interest).

developer's risk and profit In a residual valuation the amount which is allowed to cover both: a) an estimate of the sum needed to reflect the risk element between the valuation date and the completion of the development program; and b) an amount to meet the developer's requirement for profit on the venture.

development application (DA) An application to the local authority for any development concerned with establishing the principle of a proposed land use — as opposed to the details of a particular building which is the subject of the building application.

development charge/differential premium (*SGP*) A levy imposed when planning permission is granted to carry out development on a site for a more intensive use; change of use or higher plot ratio. Development charges are applicable to freehold land while differential premium is generally more applicable for the removal of restrictions on leasehold properties.

development control (*SGP*) The implementation and enforcement of planning standards by the Urban Redevelopment Authority.

Development Guide Plans (DGP) (*SGP*) These are blueprints which map out the future physical development of specific areas. For purposes of planning, Singapore is divided into 55 planning areas. A DGP is prepared for each planning area where the broad vision of the Concept Plan is translated into specific land-use proposals like land use and density. Together, the 55 DGPs form the Master Plan.

dian (典權) (*TWN*) The right to use a real property of another person and to collect profits therefrom by paying the price for the dian and taking possession of the real property for a period not exceeding 30 years.

Dinas Tata Kota (*IDN*) Town Planning Authority.

direct property Direct ownership and/or control of physical property.

direct vacancy Vacant space which is available for lease directly from the property owner.

disclaimer The renunciation of: 1) a right or claim; 2) an interest in property, e.g., the liquidator of a company may disclaim an onerous lease held by the company; 3) a possible obligation or responsibility, e.g., in a survey report the renunciation of responsibility for the consequences of non-notification of defects in inaccessible parts of a building.

disclosure Making information available, especially to the public, as in the case of a quoted company producing and distributing a detailed and comprehensive report usually each year, which presents a true and fair picture of its financial position (capital and revenue) and of the activities undertaken during the period under review. Public opinion has, over the years, called for less secrecy, more accountability and more openness in the type, breadth and depth of information which is disclosed. The underlying reason is to minimize the risk of dishonest or otherwise improper conduct of business affairs. The more open a company or country is, the more transparent it is said to be.

discount rate The rate adopted to capitalize net cash flows to come up with the capital value. The rate could be adopted by making reference to the cost of capital or the opportunity cost of the investment capital.

discount store A store that sells well known brands at discounted prices.

discount store (discount warehouse) A retail outlet which, because it is one of many branches belonging to the same owner who is able to buy goods in bulk, can offer them at a relatively low price. Unlike the practice in traditional multiple shops, the price charged to retail customers reflects a proportion of the preferential discount available to the store owner.

discounted cash flow analysis A method of computation to arrive at the present value of cash flows that are expected in future.

discounting Method for reducing a future cash flow to account for the time value of money.

discovery of documents The compulsory disclosure of relevant documents held by one party to the opposing party in a civil action or arbitration.

dissolution The scrapping of an agreement or a partnership.

distress sale Sale of property in order to raise acutely needed cash.

distributed load Weight that is distributed over a given area.

district An administrative area smaller than a state.

district plan (*NZL*) A document, generally consisting of maps, policies and rules which sets out the activities permitted on any land governed by a district or city council.

ditch Narrow, shallow channel.

divest To sell.

divided interest The interest of different people, like owner, tenant, mortgage holder, etc., in the same property.

dividend Share of income that is distributed to shareholders.

dividend yield Absolute returns expressed as a percentage of total investment.

division wall Wall that separates two buildings or rooms.

DIY (do-it-yourself) store An outlet mainly supplying the retail buyer (usually a householder) with basic materials, components and goods to be used for building, plumbing, furnishing, decorating, etc. Often these outlets are located on the periphery of a town, with on-site parking space, and maybe established in suitably adapted warehouses or other buildings with adequate clear space.

domicile Legal term indicating the place or country in which one is permanently resident.

dominant estate Land which does not have access to a public road which is given a right of way through an adjoining land.

dosi gyehok-se (*KOR*) City planning tax. Persons who own land or houses within area announced by the mayor or country commissioner as an area for the assessment of city planning tax are liable to pay tax on the value of the land or house at a rate of 0.2% or 0.3%.

double (room) occupancy, percentage of Total occupancy of double rooms in a hotel expressed as a percentage of total room nights available.

double glazing Window having two glass panes with air in between for improved thermal and sound insulation.

down payment A sum of money, which is part of the purchase price, paid immediately when the option to a property purchase is exercised.

downtown The main business hub of a city.

draft curtains Fire-proof material attached to the roof or walls of a building that stop fires in one section spreading to others.

drainage System for carrying liquid wastes away from an area.

drawdown Part of a construction loan that is released on the achievement of pre-determined milestones.

driveway Private road leading from a road or public place up to a house.

dry mortgage A mortgage in which the mortgagor has no personal liability. The mortgaged property is the only security.

dry-wall construction Construction technique in which little or no water is used in the erection of the walls inside a building. Pre-fabricated or other sheets are used for these walls.

dual agency An agent who represents and is paid commissions or consideration by both buyer and seller.

dual-use apartment Apartment that can be used as both residential and small office or shop.

ducts A conduit for the passage of electric wires, liquids or gas from one part of a building to another.

due date The date on which the rent is due and payable to the landlord.

duplex Building with two residential units, or a house or apartment spanning two floors.

dutch auction An auction at which the proceedings commence with the auctioneer quoting a higher price than he might reasonably expect to receive. If he is unable to secure an acceptance at that figure he will reduce the figure by stages until someone accepts. The acceptor is then legally obliged to proceed with the purchase.

dwelling unit (dwelling house) House or apartment where one resides.

earnest money A sum deposited, before an agreement is binding in law, by one of the parties with the other as an indication of his good faith and his intention to honor the terms of the agreement, e.g., a pre-contract deposit.

easement The right, either expressed or implied, that one has over another person's property.

eaves That part of a roof that extends beyond the walls of a building.

EBITDA Earnings before interest, tax, depreciation and amortization.

economic life The time during which an asset continues to give financial returns.

economic obsolescence The decline in value of a property due to its condition.

economic rent Market value of rent at a given point of time.

economical housing A relatively cheap apartment catering to families or individuals with lower incomes, in which the price is dominated or guided by the government.

effective age The estimation of the age of a building based on its condition, and not chronological age. Obviously, better maintained buildings will have a lower effective age than others.

effective rent Actual rent plus other expenses like maintenance and other service charges that increase the total outgoing for the tenant.

effective rental Rental paid by a tenant after taking into account incentives offered in the leasing of space.

effluent Liquid industrial, urban or human waste that flows through sewers.

egress The action of leaving or exiting a property. Also means the right to use another person's land or property.

elevation The view of the frontal façade of a building, or the height of a place above sea level.

eminent domain Right of the state or any of its instrumentalities to take private property for public use upon payment of just compensation.

encroachment Unauthorized extension of the boundaries of a piece of land over adjoining land which belongs to another.

encumbrance, incumbrance Claims or liens on a building or property.

end loan The post-completion loan on a property.

endorsement, indorsement The transfer of a note or check by the holder of the same to another by the act of signing on the back of the said instrument.

entire agreement An agreement that includes the attached exhibits/ annexures and constitutes the entire agreement between the landlord and the tenant with respect to the demised premises.

entity A separate identity, as of a company or body corporate.

entrance The point of entry into a house, room, compound or enclosed area.

environment The area surrounding a property.

environmental heritage Those features of the environment (both natural and manmade) which are considered worthy of statutory protection.

environmental impact report Study on the impact of a project on the environment of an area or a region.

environmental laws Means all central, state and local statutes regulations and ordinances and/or notification relating to the regulation or protection of the environment or health or safety.

equity linked mortgage A title deed of a property that is held as a mortgage without any transfer of title.

equivalent yield It is a weighted average of the initial yield and reversionary yield and represents the return a property will produce based upon the timing of the income received. In accordance with usual practice, the equivalent yields (as determined by the group's external valuers) assume rent received annually in arrears and on gross values including prospective purchasers, cost.

escalation clause A clause in a lease agreement or an agreement for sale providing for an increase in rent or an increase in the price of an apartment or building in the event of certain event or events happening.

escheat (*PHL*) Reversion of private property to the state due to the intestate death of the owner who does not have any legal heir; or confiscation of illegally acquired property.

escrow A deed which is signed, sealed and conditionally delivered but does not become operative until the condition has been fulfilled. In the meantime it is usually held by a third party.

estate 1) An interest held in land. Such interest is generally classified as either freehold or leasehold. 2) In common usage, synonymous with land e.g. estate agent.

estate agent One who acts for, and usually advises, a principal in respect of transactions involving real estate, e.g., sales purchases, lettings, etc.

estimated useful life The period of time over which the owner of an asset estimates that that asset will continue to be of productive use or have continuing value.

ex gratia As a favor, i.e., something done without legal obligation or admission of liability.

ex gratia payment A discretionary payment, usually one made to a payee who has no strict entitlement to compensation.

excavate To dig up the earth in order to reveal what lies beneath.

exception Exclusions in an insurance policy.

excess rent Rents which are greater than the fair rental value of a property.

exchange of contracts The first formal and legally enforceable step in the disposal of real property, i.e., when the parties duly sign and exchange copies of a document embodying the terms of the deal.

exclusive agency agreement An agreement that prohibits a principal from appointing more than one agent. An agreement that gives an agent exclusive rights to deal on behalf of a principal.

exclusive listing Contract between principal and broker wherein the former agrees to pay the latter a certain sum of money regardless of whether the latter plays a role in the execution of the transaction.

execute To complete a transaction.

execution The act of signing a document in such a way as to make it legally enforceable. In the case of a deed this is achieved in the time-honored way of signing (in the presence of witnesses), sealing and delivering.

executive condominiums (ECs) (*SGP*) These are strata-titled apartments built by the private sector and have facilities comparable to private condominiums. However, there are some restrictions attached to it in the initial years such as eligibility conditions and minimum occupation period before it can be sold.

executor The person appointed by a testator (maker of a will) to carry out instructions contained therein.

expansion option Lessee's right to take additional space within the building.

expenses Costs.

expenses of sale Cost of services required for selling an asset.

expert testimony Evidence or testimony given by a person who is an expert in that field.

expert witness A person with special experience, knowledge of or skills in a subject whom a court will accept as such and allow to attest to facts and give an opinion.

export processing zones Established specifically for the manufacture and export of finished product designed for export.

exposure Extent to which a property is brought to public notice through advertising. Also, the extent of financial involvement in a project.

express condition (*MYS*) A condition created and explicitly stated within a land title stipulating the condition of the use of a land.

expropriation Eminent domain or nationalization.

extended coverage Insurance term meaning coverage that extends beyond that provided by a standard policy.

extension The continuation of an agreement under existing terms and conditions.

extension of mortgage The extension of a mortgage.

extension of time An agreed addition to the activity or project program due to a delay (may or may not have cost implications).

exterior The outside of a building.

exterior finish The outside facing of a building.

exterior wall Outer wall of a building that is exposed to the atmosphere.

external valuer For the purpose of asset valuations, a qualified valuer who is not an internal valuer and where neither he nor any of his partners or co-directors are directors or employees of the company or another company within a group of companies or have a significant financial interest in the company or group, or where neither the company nor the group has a significant financial interest in the valuer's firm or company.

F

FIP Fire Indicator Panel that identifies to building management and fire brigade where alarms have occurred.

FIT It is an acronym with multiple meanings: foreign individual traveler, frequent individual traveler, or fully independent traveler. FIT often applies to an international pre-paid unescorted tour that includes several travel elements such as accommodations, rental cars, and sightseeing.

FOC An acronym for free of charge. Includes any goods or services provided gratis.

façade The front face of a building.

face rent The quoted rent without taking out the effect of rent-free periods, rebates or incentives, if any.

face rental Nominal gross market rental as represented on a lease.

facilities management The management of owned and occupied corporate real estate and the services provided for the occupants.

facility The building or area constructed specifically to accommodate the occupiers' needs.

fair market value The amount at which an item could be exchanged between willing unrelated parties, other than in a forced liquidation. It is usually the quoted market price when a market exists for the item.

fair rent The market rent of a property.

far (*THA*) Plot ratio or the building to land ratio.

fee Remuneration paid to a professional adviser or real estate agent.

fee simple 1) The highest form of freehold land tenure under English law, in which "fee" signifies heritability of the tenancy and "simple" that there is no qualification as to the heirs who may succeed to do it. 2) Commonly, though wrongly, used as a synonym for freehold tenure, which has a wider meaning in law.

fengshui Feng Shui or fengshui is the ancient Chinese practice of placement and arrangement of space to achieve harmony with the environment. The practice is estimated to be more than 3,000 years old. It is also known as geomancy and is still actively practiced and observed by individuals and companies in many parts of Asia, especially in Hong Kong and China.

FF&E Furniture, fittings and equipment not fixed to the structure that are required in the fit out of a facility (commonly used in hotel construction i.e., beds, lamps, desk, etc.).

final account The agreed amount to be paid to the contractor/s for works completed including any adjustments for variations, delay costs, etc.

final completion The date following the defects liability period when a project is deemed complete and all final payments have been paid.

financing costs The rate of interest and other service charges needed to obtain a loan.

finder's fee A fee paid to an unlicensed broker for an introduction.

fire sprinkler system A system installed in the ceiling of buildings that automatically sprinkle water (in order to douse flames) if the ambient temperature crosses a given threshold.

fire wall Wall that prevents fire from spreading to other parts of a building.

firm commitment An irrevocable and legally binding statement agreeing to do or not do something.

first mortgage The mortgage that has priority over all others when there is a second charge on the mortgaged asset.

first partial month's payment If the rent commencement date for the first month of the initial term is other than the first day of a calendar month, then the rent for such partial month is prorated on daily basis, based on the actual number of days in such calendar month.

first refusal right A right given by one party to another whereby the first party is obliged to give the second party a chance to acquire an asset before he offers it to anyone else.

first-level market The land market where developers obtain land from the government via auction or bid.

first-tier city（一级城市）(*CHN*) Cities that are first market entry-points for most foreign companies. Its office markets have quality facilities, professional property management, and its markets have a degree of sophistication in property purchasing and leasing. These are generally said to be Beijing, Guangzhou, Shanghai and Shenzhen.

fit-out The physical components included in a facility constructed to enable the occupier to utilize the space.

fit-out costs Expenses incurred in fitting out premises prior to occupancy.

fit-out period Period wherein lessee may perform fit-out works.

fittings Items which are affixed to land or buildings and which are easily removed.

fixed assets Assets of a permanent nature the benefit of which is expected to be enjoyed beyond the current financial year.

fixed price contract A building contract in which the total price is fixed at the outset usually subject only to changes due to subsequent variations in statutory undertakers' charges.

fixed rate mortgage A mortgage where the rate of interest remains constant throughout.

fixed rent A rent which cannot be changed during the entire period of a lease or, at the date when the lease is being valued, will be unaltered for such a length of time that no change in capital value would be attributed to the prospect of a different rent during the remainder of the lease.

fixtures Items that are fixed to property and treated as part of that property. Unless specifically excluded, sale of property includes the sale of fixtures as well.

flagship store A large, signature store that showcases the best and widest variety of merchandise for a particular brand. It may serve as a mini-anchor in a shopping mall or may take the form of an iconic standalone building.

flat A separate set of premises, normally all on the same floor, forming part of a building, divided horizontally from some other part of the building, constructed or adapted for the purposes of a private dwelling and occupied wholly or mainly as a private dwelling.

flat lease An agreement where the same amount of rent has to be paid throughout the life of a lease.

flatted factory A high-rise industrial building that accommodates light industry that is non-pollutive. It may be located close to residential areas because of its non-pollutive nature.

flexible interest rate Same as variable interest rate and flexible interest rate. A rate that can move up and down between due payment, as opposed to a fixed interest rate that is set for the life of the loan or a predetermined period.

floating charge A charge where the lender has security for a loan spread over all, or a defined class of, the borrower's assets.

floor area The aggregate superficial area of a building, taking each floor into account.

floor load The live or superimposed load on a floor, usually expressed in pounds per square foot (lb/sq. ft.) or kilo-Newtons per square meter (kN/m_).

floor plan An architectural sketch of various rooms, balconies, bathrooms, etc.

floor space The total area covered by a building. It includes external walls, partitions, stairwells, plant rooms and enclosed car parking areas.

floor space index (FSI) The quotient of the ratio of the combined gross floor area of all floors, to the total area of the plot.

floor space ratio (FSR) (*AUS*) Similar to the definition of plot ratio, it describes the relationship between land area and permissible gross floor space allowable under the local planning code.

flowage easement An easement by convention that allows water from lands at higher levels to flow into and through lands located at lower levels even though there may be no agreements to such effect.

force majeure An act of god (natural calamities), or an act of man (war, riots) beyond the control of the parties to a contract which makes it impossible for one of the parties to fulfill the terms of that contract. Many contracts have a force majeure clause.

forced sale Sale, which is made without the voluntary consent of the owner, such as when properties are sold for defaults on loans.

foreclosure The act of taking away the right, title and interest of the owner of a property or asset in default of due payments.

foreclosure sale The sale of a property following foreclosure.

foreign investor Investor who purchases/sells property in an overseas jurisdiction.

forfeit The loss of a right, privilege, property, or money because of a crime, breach of obligation, or neglect of duty.

franchise A system of business in which a company is owned by one or more persons, but other people are allowed to use its name and good will to sell some centrally approved products and services in return for a franchise fee. Franchise agreements often make it mandatory for franchisees (persons taking a franchise) to buy certain items from the franchisors.

fraud An act that is done with the intent of acquiring property or money by deceit.

free and clear Property that is not encumbered.

free standing building A standalone building which is not attached to any other building.

freehold A tenure in perpetuity.

front elevation Height. Also means frontal face of a building.

full house A hundred per cent occupancy in a commercial or residential property or hotel.

full rental value (FRV) The best possible rental that might reasonably be expected in the open market for a particular property at a given time, having regard to the terms of the actual or notional lease, e.g., responsibility for repairs rights of assignment or subletting, or basis of review.

functional obsolescence Something that is no longer useful because it is outdated, though it may still have some residual economic life.

funding Commonly used to refer to the financing of property development.

furniture and fixtures Accounting term covering furniture and other items that are used in an office or home but not part of the property.

G

ga-deunggi (*KOR*) Provisional registration.

gamjung (*KOR*) Real estate valuation (or appraisal).

gap financing Temporary financing to bridge the difference between the construction loan and the permanent loan.

garage 1) A building or indoor area for parking or storing motor vehicles. 2) A commercial establishment for repairing and servicing motor vehicles.

garden apartments A low-rise apartment building or building complex surrounded by lawns and trees, shrubbery, or gardens.

gazebo 1) A structure, as an open or latticework pavilion or summerhouse, built on a site that provides an attractive view. 2) A small roofed structure that is screened on all sides, used for outdoor entertaining and dining.

gazumping A situation in which a vendor, having agreed to sell property at a certain price subject to contract, breaks his word and either seeks a higher price from the purchaser on the grounds of having received a higher offer from another or accepts a higher offer from another.

gearing 1) The use of borrowed money to generate a higher yield through investment in real estate. 2) The relationship between a company's loan capital and its equity capital. This is usually expressed as the ratio of loan capital to net asset value.

general contractor Contractor who assumes responsibility for completing a construction project, under contract to the owner, and hires, supervises and pays all subcontractors.

general lien A lien that includes all property of the debtor rather than a specific property.

general mortgage A mortgage that includes all real property of the mortgagor, both what he has and what he may acquire in future.

general partner The managing partner of a limited partnership who is in charge of its operations and has unlimited liability. A limited partnership must have one general partner. All partners in an ordinary partnership are general partners.

gentleman's agreement An agreement, usually not in writing, that is not legally enforceable but intended to rest on the honor of parties.

geomancer One who practices geomancy, fengshui.

gerrymander To make manmade boundaries that go against the natural scheme of things. For example: to create a new geographical constituency against tradition and natural sub-divisions to exclude certain castes, classes or categories of people in order to create an electorate that helps a particular candidate or political party.

gross floor area (GFA) The area to be leased is usually quoted on the basis of gross floor area, which includes not only the gross area of the leased floor but also portions of common areas. The ratio of "net lettable area" to GFA varies, naturally depending on the efficiency of the superstructure and the area of the basement levels included in GFA calculations.

gift tax A tax imposed on gifts of money, property or goods.

going concern value The total value of a business as carried on, with all its assets and liabilities, good will and potentialities. If the premises used are owned by the business, they form part of the going concern value on the basis of their value to the business.

gongdong shisul-se (_KOR_) Community facility tax. Persons benefiting from the provision of fire service facilities, garbage disposal, sewerage, or similar facilities are subject to a tax of 0.06% - 0.16%.

good class bungalows (_SGP_) These are large size detached houses with a minimum plot size of 1,400 sq. m. They are found in the 39 designated bungalow zones in Singapore.

good faith Transaction done with good intention, honesty, fairness without deceit and with honorable intention.

good will An intangible asset that represents the excess of the amount paid for an acquired company over the fair market value of the net assets of that company. Basically, it is the value of the name, reputation and brand of the acquired company.

government announced land value (公告地價) (*TWN*) A land value used by municipalities to compute land value tax; it is assessed once every three years by municipalities. The value is much lower than the market value.

government rates (差餉) (*HKG*) Rates are a tax on the occupation of property, and are charged at a percentage of the rateable value of property. The current percentage is 5% (2006).

government rent (地租) (*HKG*) The rent payable by the land owner to the government under the land lease. The government rent could be a lump sum rent or 3% of the rateable value of the property, depending on the type of the land lease.

grace period A period of time after a payment such as a loan or insurance premium, becomes due, before one is subject to penalties, late charges, forfeiture or cancellation.

grade 1) The degree or rise of a sloping surface. 2) To change the original slope of ground to prepare for paving or for drainage purposes. 3) Classification of building quality. In Asia Pacific property markets, top tier property is termed Premium or A Grade.

gradient The degree of inclination, or the rate of ascent or descent of a surface.

graduated lease A lease where the rental is not fixed and may vary according to value arrived on periodic appraisal.

grandfather clause A clause in the legislation that allows the continuation of a business, practice, activity, etc., that was permitted by legislation but currently considered not permissible by a change in the legislation.

grant A term that refers to a transfer of property by deed or the property so transferred.

grant deed A deed, conveying property owned by an individual or a company, to another individual or a company. Contains clauses that secure it against any prior conveyances or encumbrances.

gravel Particles of rock, i.e., stones and pebbles, usually round in form and intermediate in size between sand grains and boulders which is used extensively in building roads and in making concrete.

graveyard A private or public plot of land used as a burial ground or a cemetery.

green field site A site, separate from existing developments, which is to be developed for the first time.

grid 1) A pattern of lines laid out at right angles to each other. 2) A series of intersecting lines dividing a map or chart into equal sections. 3) The intersecting bars, wires, or supports as in a grating or supports in a dropped ceiling. 4) A network of pipes for the distribution of water or gas. 5) A chart used by insurance companies and lenders for rating property, risk of the borrower, neighborhood, etc.

gross Without deductions. Total, as the amount of sales, salary, profit, etc., before taking deductions for expenses, taxes, or the like.

gross activity The total level of space leased or occupied between two points in time.

gross area The total floor area of a structure, in square feet or square meters, measured from the outside.

gross development value (*HKG*) The aggregate capital value of the stratified units of the proposed development assuming completion of construction as at the date of assessment.

gross effective income Expected income from all operations after an allowance for vacancies and an allowance for collection losses is deducted.

gross external area (GEA) Formerly referred to as "reduced cover area" or "gross floor space." The aggregate superficial area of a building taking each floor into account. This includes: external walls and projections; internal wall and partitions; columns and piers.

gross floor area The total of all covered areas including common areas such as amenities and parking.

gross income Total income before expenses and taxes are subtracted.

gross lease A lease in which the lessor pays all costs of operation. A gross lease is a lease at a fixed amount allowing the lessee to know exactly how much rent will be due and payable each period during the term of the lease. The lessor pays all taxes, insurance, and maintenance on the property.

gross operating profit Gross receipts less the cost of goods or production but before the deduction of indirect cost or expenses such as rent, salaries, etc.

gross rent Refers to the total rentals payable by tenants. This is equivalent to the sum of net rent plus outgoings.

gross sales The total sales, for a specific period, before adjusting discounts or returns.

ground beam A horizontal reinforced concrete beam for supporting walls, joists, etc., at or near ground level, itself either resting directly upon the ground or supported at both ends by piers.

ground lease A lease of land, as opposed to a lease of a building.

ground level At surface level.

ground rent The rent paid by a lessee for the use of land.

ground water Water beneath the earth's surface, often between saturated soil and rock that supplies wells and springs.

grounds Large natural ground level adjoining or around a structure.

guarantor A person who makes or gives a guarantee.

guaranty An agreement by which one person assumes responsibility for paying another's debts or fulfilling another's responsibilities.

gubun deunggi (*KOR*) Strata-title (partial ownership of the building). Based on the concept of the horizontal and vertical sub-division of airspace enabling land and buildings to be sub-divided into lots with a separate individual title to each lot. The ownership and management of multi-unit buildings are regulated, through which the creation of an agent management body is required. As "agent" for the proprietors of the multi-building unit lots, the body is responsible for the maintenance and management of the building.

gunmul deunggi (*KOR*) Building title.

gunpye-rul (rate) (*KOR*) The building-to-land ratio.

gutter Manmade ditch, usually paved, which carries rainwater and other waste water out of an area.

gwanribee (*KOR*) Service charges (maintenance fees). This includes air conditioning, electricity for common areas, security, gas, taxes, insurance and other services (varies throughout market). Payable in addition to chonsei and walsei amounts.

gyouk-se (*KOR*) Education tax. This is payable by the taxpayer of Property Tax and Aggregated Land Tax pursuant to the Local Tax Law at a rate of 20% of the Property Tax and Aggregated Land Tax.

habitable room Room that is fit for living in. the building in which the room is located conforms to the building code and has a certificate of occupancy. Usable for all purposes, but does not include facility rooms such as a bathroom, closets, or storage rooms.

Hak Guna Bangunan (HGB) (*IDN*) Most common title, typically a leasehold of 20 to 30 years and extendable.

Hak Guna Usaha (*IDN*) Right of Exploitation.

Hak Milik (*IDN*) Equivalent to freehold interest.

Hak Pakai (*IDN*) Right of Use.

Hak Pengelolaan (*IDN*) Right to Operate.

Hak Pengelolaan Lahan (*IDN*) Right to manage land, generally granted to government entities.

hall 1) A corridor or passageway in a building. 2) The large entrance room of a house or building; vestibule; lobby. 3) A large room or building for public gatherings.

hamlet A small village.

handover condition Condition of the office unit/premises upon turn-over to the lessee.

hard option (*IND*) Option on a certain area of premises (i.e., 100 sq. ft. or 1,000 sq. ft. or 100,000 sq. ft.) offered by the lessor to the lessee over a fixed duration of time where in the lessor will not market the area to another tenant/party for that specific time frame. A hard option can either be free of cost or could have a holding cost of a bear minimum value.

hardware The metal accessories used in construction such as doorknobs, hinges, locks, etc.

HDB flats (*SGP*) Public housing built by the Housing & Development Board (HDB). Majority (more than 80%) of Singaporeans stay in HDB flats.

headline rent See "face rent."

heads of terms A document signed between the lessor and lessee or the buyer and seller which outlines the commercial terms agreed upon and usually provides a date and duration by which the final agreement is to be executed. Such a document does not create any legal obligation on either party until and unless some monetary value has been paid to the seller or lessor.

heavy industry Any industry which is capital and/or labor-intensive designated "heavy industry" under a zoning ordinance such as automobile, industrial machinery, steel, rubber, mining or petroleum.

hectare A measurement, equaling 2.471 acres or about 107,637 square feet or 10,000 square meters.

hedge Investment with the characteristic that the investor's capital and/or income is to varying degrees protected from loss due to inflation or other causes of price movement from inflationary effects. As with a natural hedge, which reduces the impact of wind and provides shelter, it cannot act as a complete barrier in gale force conditions. The financial crisis throughout the world in the early 1970s uprooted many financial "hedges," as did the one in 1987 and the Asian financial crisis in 1997.

high-end apartment An apartment that is more luxurious than a standard apartment, but does not have all of the amenities and facilities to be a "luxury apartment."

highest and best use Appraisal term meaning the possible use of a property that would produce the greatest net income and thereby develop the highest value.

high-rise apartment building An apartment building having a comparatively large number of stories, considered "high" in the area where it is built and equipped with elevators.

high-scale apartment Refers to high-end apartments and luxury apartments.

historical cost Original cost of an asset at the time of purchase or payment as opposed to its saleable value, replacement value or present value.

hi-tech building (high-technology building) Primarily a modern industrial building that is particularly suited to the flexible uses and space needs of business organizations engaged in modern technologies. Such activities require more column-free office or laboratory space than a traditional factory and also more sophisticated and adaptable installations for services and communications.

hold over tenant A term for a tenant who continues to retain possession of a property after the expiry of the lease.

holding cost (*IND*) A fixed amount paid to the lessor for a predefined time frame (i.e., hard options period).

holding period The length of time an asset was held, that is, the time between the trade date of the purchase and the trade date of the sale.

home financing Loans for the construction of single or multi-family dwellings by banks or other such lending institutions.

horizon The line or circle that forms the apparent boundary between earth and sky, when viewed from a distance. Also refers to layers of soil such as "A" horizon, "B" horizon, etc.

hoshokin / shikikin (*JPN*) Security deposit. A monetary deposit paid to the lessor by the lessee, usually several months' rent amount CAM charge not included, to be returned at the termination of lease. As a form of guarantee, it can be used to offset any debt by the lessee, such as payment delinquency.

hot-desking A desk sharing system for employees in an office increasingly used by tenants whose employees are regularly out of the office to reduce space requirement.

hotel A commercial establishment offering lodging to travelers and sometimes to permanent residents, and often having restaurants, meeting rooms, stores, etc., that are available to the general public.

hotelling A space usage term. Employees have no designated desk and select available desks on a daily use basis.

house A building in which people live or a residential structure.

house tax (房屋稅) (*TWN*) A building tax is levied based on the current value of standard price and applicable tax rate, not based on the building cost or market value. It is calculated by the following formula: Standard House Price x Size (acreage) x (1 - an Applicable Depreciation Rate x the Years of Depreciation) x an Adjustment Rate based on the Level / Class of Street or Road x an Applicable Tax Rate = Payable House Tax.

Housing & Development Board (HDB) (*SGP*) HDB is Singapore's public housing authority. It plans and develops public housing towns that provide Singaporeans with affordable, quality homes and living environments.

Housing Developer Sale License (SL) (*SGP*) This is the sale license issued by the Comptroller of Housing to enable developers to develop and sell residential projects before their completion. Sales can only start after obtaining the sale license and the building plan approval.

housing starts A measure of actual commencement of construction of houses, condominiums, and apartment construction. Permits are considered a leading indicator of housing starts.

hutong (胡同) (*CHN*) Traditional Chinese neighborhood, in which pingfang or courtyards are connected by walls.

hypermarket A large (50,000 to 200,000 sq. ft.) low-rise retail centre which sells a wide range of food and general merchandise at low prices. Typically located on a large tract of land off highways or major roads or in suburban locations. However in certain land-scarce cities (such as Singapore or parts of China), they may be located within a shopping mall and function as an anchor tenant of the mall.

Ijin Mendirikan Bangunan (IMB) (*IDN*) Building permit (all buildings should have this permit).

imdae cha (*KOR*) Lease.

immovable Things which cannot be moved, such as land, buildings, etc.

implied Something apparent from the circumstances, rather than from direct action or communication.

implied contract An agreement created by actions of the parties involved but not written or spoken.

improved land Land that has been developed for use and has had installation of such utilities as water, sewer, roads and building structures. These improvements make the raw land increase its usability, thereby increasing the market value.

improved value An assessment term that comprises of the total value of land along with improvements, instead of the separate values of each.

improvements Generally, physical changes which enhance the capital value of land or buildings. These may include additional buildings, extensions to existing buildings, installation of new services, e.g., central heating and air conditioning and infrastructure works. On the other hand, mere replacement by a modern equivalent of something worn out would normally be regarded as a repair rather than improvement.

in perpetuity Of endless duration; forever.

inbreng (*IDN*) Contribution in kind.

incentive An inducement offered by a landlord to a potential tenant. Can take several forms including contribution to fit-out costs or rent free periods.

incinerator A heavily insulated, furnace-like device for burning rubbish, giving off a minimum of heat and smoke, and burning the rubbish more completely than an open fire.

inclement weather Rain, snow or other adverse weather conditions that impact on the construction of a project and may lead to a delay and or an extension of time.

income 1) Money or other benefits coming from the use of property, skill or business. 2) The excess of revenue over expenses and losses for an accounting period. 3) Any increase in the assets of a person or corporation caused by labor, sales, or return on invested funds.

incorporate To constitute into a corporation recognized by law, with special functions, rights, duties and liabilities; as, to incorporate a bank, a company, a club, a society, etc. To create a corporation.

increment 1) The small quantity by which a variable increases or is increased. 2) A negative increment is a decrease. 3) The fact of becoming greater or larger.

incubation space (*IND*) Fully fitted out interim space offered by the lessor/ developers to the lessee/tenant for a short duration of three to 12 months till the permanent space/building is ready and operational. Sometimes available in Science Parks and Business Parks to assist or encourage research & development start-ups or to nurture small businesses.

incumbrance (encumbrance) Claim or lien or interest in a property that complicates the title process, interfering with its use or transfer. Restrictive covenants.

indemnity agreement 1) An agreement whereby one party agrees to secure another against an anticipated loss or damage. For example, someone may agree to turn a business over to another person for a reduced price if he pays the debts and other obligations of the business. In a broad sense, insurance policies are indemnity contracts. 2) A provision in a lease that requires a tenant to pay (indemnify) a landlord for damages.

indenture Written agreement between two or more persons having different interests.

independent appraisal Value estimate provided by someone who has no participation in ownership of the property in question.

independent contractor One who is hired to do a particular job and is subject to the direction of the person in charge. Independent contractors pay for their own expenses and taxes and are not viewed as employees with benefits.

independent expert Someone with relevant specialist knowledge who is appointed to resolve a difference between parties, e.g., a rent review or the interpretation of a clause in a lease. They use their own specialist knowledge in addition to any evidence presented to them. Their decision is final and binding on the parties but, unless their contract of appointment provides otherwise, they can be sued by an aggrieved party if their decisions are manifestly negligent.

index lease A rental contract in which the tenant's rental is tied to a change in a price index.

indexing To alter mortgage term, payment, or rate according to inflation and/or a suitable mortgage rate index.

indirect lighting Lighting that has a large portion of emitted light directed upward, often off a ceiling, before shining on an area or object. It reduces glare in the area being lighted and creates fewer shadows.

indirect property Indirect ownership of property, the most common form being shares in a REIT (real estate investment trust) whose underlying assets are physical property.

indorsement (endorsement) A signature on a draft or check by a payee prior to the transfer to a third party. Also, a statement attached to an insurance policy, which changes the terms of the policy.

industrial / office building (*HKG*) A dual-purpose building in which every unit of the building can be used flexibly for both industrial and office purposes. In terms of building construction, the building must comply with all relevant building and fire regulations applicable to both industrial and office buildings, including floor loading, compartmentation, lighting, ventilation, provision of means of escape and sanitary fitments.

industrial estate (*HKG*) In the three industrial estates in Hong Kong, The Hong Kong Science and Technology Park offers developed land at cost to both manufacturing and service industries with new or improved technology and processes which cannot operate in multi-storey factory or commercial buildings.

industrial park An area zoned and planned for the purpose of industrial development. Usually located outside the main residential area of a city and normally provided with adequate transportation access, including roads and rail.

industrial property Property that is zoned and used for industrial use, such as factories, manufacturing, research and development, warehouse space and industrial parks.

inflation Increasing price levels. A loss in the purchasing power of money.

infrastructure Apparatus, buildings, and structures providing essential services to any real estate development. Includes roads, water, gas, telephone, electricity, broadband, etc.

ingress and egress Access from a land parcel to a public road or other means of exit. Right to enter and exit through land owned by another.

inheritance tax State tax based on the value of property and other assets received through inheritance.

initial public offering (IPO) First offering of units in a vehicle to the public, for example, shares offered with the floating of a REIT.

initial return In an investment analysis, the initial net income at the date of purchase expressed as a percentage of the purchase price.

initial term Described in the agreement as the initial period for which the demised premise has been taken up on lease. Usually for a period of three years or 36 months.

initial yield The percentage return on price or value derived from the current net passing income. This is the ratio between the initial income and price or capital value, expressed as a percentage. No allowance is made for any future rental growth.

injunction A court order issued to a defendant in an action either prohibiting or commanding the performance of a defined act. Violation of an injunction could lead to a contempt of court citation.

Inland Revenue Authority of Singapore (IRAS) (*SGP*) Acts as an agent of the government and provides services in administering, assessing, collecting and enforcing payment of taxes.

inner city The central core of a city, which generally includes the older and more urbanized sections. It contains the major commercial center, termed the central business district.

installment contract / sale Purchase agreement where the buyer does not receive title to the property until all installments are paid. Transaction in which the sale price is paid in installments. The tax is calculated on these sales on the basis of profit made by the seller per installment received and may be paid over the installment period.

institutional lenders Financial intermediaries, who invest in loans and other securities on behalf of their depositors or customers e.g., insurance company.

institutional property Property such as schools, colleges, hospitals, universities, etc.

insurable value The value of property on which the insurance is calculated.

insurance Policies that guarantee compensation for losses from a specific cause. Various forms of insurance cover against fire, flood, earthquake, liability, etc.

intangible assets Nonphysical assets with continuing value, such as good will, copyrights, trademarks and franchises.

intangible property Nonphysical valuables, such as contracts or mortgages, employee loyalty or customer good will, which are distinguished from physical property such as buildings and land.

integrated resort (IR) (*SGP*) These are integrated projects comprising entertainment and convention facilities, hotels, theme attractions, cultural amenities as well as a casino component. Singapore's two

IRs are expected to be completed in 2009-2010. One is located on Sentosa Island while the other is located in the Marina Bayfront.

interest Payments by borrowers of funds to compensate lenders for the use of their funds.

interest coverage The number of times the annual interest on debt obligations is covered by income for the year before considering interest on the debt obligations and income taxes.

interest-free security deposit A security deposit kept with the landlord by the tenant on which no interest can be claimed by the tenant from the landlord.

interest-only mortgage A mortgage under which the principal amount borrowed is repaid in one payment while interest payments are made periodically.

interest rate The percentage of the principal amount of a loan that is charged for use of that loan. This amount determines the monthly payment.

interest-rate cap An instrument that protects the holder from rises in variable (usually) short-term interest rates. The counter-party makes a payment to the holder when an underlying interest rate (the "index" or "reference" interest rate) exceeds a specified strike rate.

interest rate collar An instrument that combines the purchase of an interest-rate cap and the sale of a "floor" to specify a range in which an interest rate will fluctuate. The instrument thereby hedges the buyer's position against a rise in the floating rate but limits the benefits of a drop in that floating rate outside the defined band — the "collar."

interim financing Financing, used for a short term, to bridge the gap between the purchase and the sale, is also called a "bridge loan." Construction loans are interim financing.

internal rate of return (IRR) (money weighted rate of return) It is a method to calculate the annual yield of a financial instrument. In investments, the IRR helps to calculate the average rate of return the investment may yield over its tenure. In lending, the IRR calculates the cost of credit over the tenure of the credit transaction.

International Grade A Office development which meets a list of Grade A criteria and is wholly owned, managed to international standards and has a superior set of tenant amenities.

interruption of services This refers to a breakdown or interruption of building services that is to be provided by the landlord to a tenant in a building – e.g. provision of electrical power and air-conditioning in an office building. In a situation whereby the interruption of services severely affects the tenant's business or operations and he suffers losses, the tenant may seek compensation or rental rebate to defray or make good his losses.

intrinsic value The value of the thing itself, rather than any special features that make its market value different.

inventory Property held for sale or to be used in the manufacture of goods held for sale.

investment Expenditure to buy property or other capital assets that generate income. Alternately, securities of real estate companies or capital assets.

investment property Real estate, such as rental properties, which generate income.

investment yield The annual percentage return which is considered to be appropriate for a specific valuation or an investment, being expressed as the ratio of annual net income (actual or estimated) to the capital value.

J

jaesan-se (*KOR*) Property tax. Payable by owners of buildings as at the base date of assessment. The tax base is the current "Standard Value" of the building as determined by the relevant local government and the tax rate varies, depending on the type of property.

janitor Care taker of a building. Generally associated with the maintenance of cleaning, locking up after closing, and minor repair work.

jeondae (*KOR*) Sub-lease.

jeonhwan-rul (rate) (*KOR*) Conversion rate chonsei to walsei. Chonsei amount can be converted to monthly rental by applying a conversion rate. These rates, ranging from 12% to 18%, are applied to obtain the conversion rate.

jeonyong-rul (rate) (*KOR*) Building efficiency rate (net to gross ratio). Critical to Korea as rental is charged based on the gross area. The tenant is responsible for paying a portion of common areas that include lift lobbies, corridors, bathrooms and stairwells.

jerry-built A construction built of inferior and cheap materials. Poor quality.

jihap gunmul (*KOR*) Multi-unit building.

joint Used to indicate a common property ownership interest in real estate. Indicates a shared liability in terms of a contractual relationship.

joint agent Two or more agents jointly instructed by a principal to act on his behalf. In the case of estate agents this is normally on the basis that if any one of the agents effects the sale, letting or other disposition of the property, being the subject of the principal's instructions, the other joint agent(s) will share the remuneration in agreed proportions.

joint and several Situation wherein each borrower, on the same note, is held fully liable for the entire amount of the debt, not just a portion. The creditor may demand full repayment from any individual.

joint sole agent One of two or more agents jointly instructed as the only agents entitled to represent the principal. It is customary for the joint agents to share any commission earned on an agreed basis, irrespective of which agent effects the sale or letting.

joint tenancy Equal ownership, by two or more people, each of whom has an undivided interest, with the right of survivorship.

joint tenants Ownership of real estate between two or more parties who have been named in one conveyance as joint tenants. Upon the death of a joint tenant, the decedent's interest passes to the surviving joint tenant or tenants by the right of survivorship.

joint venture An agreement between two or more parties to invest in a specific single business or property.

jonghap toji-se (*KOR*) Aggregated land tax. This is payable on all types of land by the owner of such land as of the base date of assessment. The tax base is the "standard value" and the general rate, which covers the most common categories of land, varies progressively from zero.

JTC Corporation (JTC) (*SGP*) JTC Corporation (JTC) is Singapore's principal developer and manager of public industrial estates and related facilities in Singapore. Over the past three decades, it has developed some 7,000 hectares of industrial land and four million square meters of ready-built factories for more than 7,000 local and multinational companies. Among these are specialized industrial parks and facilities for high-technology and biomedical industries.

judicial foreclosure Property of a defaulted borrower is sold under court order and the court ratifies the amount received.

judicial sale The sale of a property made under the order of the court through a representative appointed by the court and not the owner.

kar-nar-din (*THA*) Ground lease premium.

karn-chao-choung (*THA*) Sub-lease.

karn-oan-sitti-karn-chao (*THA*) Assignment.

kawasan industri (*IDN*) Industrial estate.

KDB (*IDN*) Site coverage ratio.

kenchiku kinjunho (*JPN*) Building Standard Law. A law that sets the minimum building standards associated with structural safety, building coverage, floor area ratio, height and fire codes for the purpose of protecting the lives, well-being and assets of the citizen and to promote social welfare.

kenpeiritsu (*JPN*) Building to land ratio.

kenrikin / reikin (*JPN*) Key money. Key money in "reikin" form varies by the region, however its origin was a token of gratitude paid to the lessor by the lessee for signing the lease. In the Kanto area, it is usually two months rent, but in Kansai there is no key money. Key money is not returned. Key money in "kenrikin" form usually applies to commercial properties, sometimes to land parcels, originally paid as a "good will" fee for operating the business in the building. It is also fundamentally non-returnable.

kios (*IDN*) Units in strata titled shopping center.

KK (kabushiki kaisha) (*JPN*) Japanese public corporation under business law.

KLB (*IDN*) Floor area ratio.

kohshin (*JPN*) Contract renewal. In essence, this is an extension of the existing lease. Without a termination notice within a period specified in the agreement, the contract is automatically renewed. Some fixed-term agreements are exceptions. Upon contract renewal for a residential property, the lessee pays a certain amount to the lessor as a "renewal fee."

koji-chika (*JPN*) Refers to the prices of land at selected sample spots in the country issued by the Ministry of Land, Infrastructure and Transport every March. It is used as an indicator for transactions as well as a benchmark for valuations.

kong-thun-ruam-asang-ha-rim-ma-sup (*THA*) Real estate investment trust.

koteishisanzei (*JPN*) Fixed Asset Tax. Fixed Asset Tax is levied on land, buildings and depreciable assets used for business purposes as of January 1st every year. Fixed Asset Tax is levied by the municipality where the fixed assets are located. The annual standard tax is 1.4%.

KPR (Kredit Pemilikan Rumah) (*IDN*) Home mortgage financing.

ku (ward) (*JPN*) Precinct unit applied in larger cities.

kubunshoyu tatemono (*JPN*) Strata Title or Partial Ownership of a Building. The ownership granted on portions that are deemed independent within a building used for residence, retail, office, warehouse, etc., whether vertical or horizontally divided.

kun-judang-kwon (*KOR*) A kun-mortgage. This is a special type of mortgage unique to Korea. It may be used to secure any type of debt. It is distinctive in that it secures the debt at its maximum amount without regard to intermediate increases or decreases in the amount of the debt. If the amount of principal outstanding plus interest at any given time falls below the secured amount, the full amount of the debt, but no more, will be secured by the mortgage. But if the amount of principal outstanding plus interest at any given time exceeds the stated maximum amount, then such excess will not be secured. Accordingly, it is advisable to fix the maximum amount at a level that exceeds the principal of the claim amount. Customarily such maximum ranges from 110-130% of the principal amount. Since a kun-mortgage is indivisible, the mortgagee may exercise its right over the whole property covered by the mortgage until its claim has been completely satisfied. Mortgagees are paid according to priority, which is generally determined at time of registration.

kunmul (*KOR*) Building.

kwonrigum (*KOR*) Premium.

kyoekihi (*JPN*) CAM charges. Fees charged on top of monthly rent of a building and its site. Generally includes water, utilities, cleaning, repair, maintenance, security and air-conditioning fees.

land Ground with all permanent overground and underground attachments like trees, minerals, etc.

land appreciation tax (土地增值税) (*CHN*) It was introduced in January 1994 and implemented in 1995.

land bank A stock of land held by a developer for future development.

land classification (土地分类) (*CHN*) According to the location of the land, the government divided the land into ten different categories, in which there is a different price for each. Land zoned for residential, commercial, industrial use will fall into one of these categories.

land grant A gift of government land to an individual or corporation.

Land Information Memorandum (LIM) (*NZL*) A report issued by a city or borough council, listing all the information that the council has about the property including what building consents and code of compliance certificates have been issued.

land owner A person or body corporate that owns the land.

land reclamation Creation of habitable land by filling up low-lying lands, wetlands, lakes or portions of the seashore.

land records The records maintained under the provisions of, or for the purposes of, the relevant land revenue code and includes a copy of maps and plans or a final town planning scheme, improvement scheme or a scheme of consolidation of holdings that has come into force in any area under any law in force.

land register sheet (土地登記簿) (*TWN*) A title deed, or land ownership certificate, includes three sections, namely: description, ownership and other rights in sequence. The cover sheet is entitled with "The Land Register or Constructional Improvements of so-and-so Township/City, District, Volume number so-and-so." Each sheet inside the register shall be affixed with the seal of land registration.

land registration (土地登記) (*TWN*) Registration of the ownership of, and other rights over, land and constructional improvements thereon. In Taiwan, land registration is carried out by the competent Special Municipality/County/City Land Office; or it is carried out by a land registry set up ad hoc in a Special Municipality/County/City by the said Land Office.

Land Titles (Strata) Act (*SGP*) This Act governs all buildings which are strata-titled. Amongst the requirements set out in the Act include the compulsory setting up of a Management Corporation (MC), application/approval for collective sale and determination of share value.

land use planning The drawing up of long-term plans for the use of land in a particular area or region.

land value increment tax (土地增值稅) (*TWN*) A property tax is levied on the basis of the net increment of the value of land, when the ownership thereof is transferred, or after the lapse of 10 full years though the ownership thereof has not been transferred. The period of 10 full years begins from the date when the value of land is assessed for the first time. Since land value increment tax is levied on realized gains from land transactions, it is sometimes imprecisely characterized as a "capital gains" tax. The formula to calculate the net increment is: Land Value Increment = Declared Present Value at the Transfer - Original Decreed Value or the Assessed Value at the Last Transfer x Consumer Price Index Adjustment - Land Improvement Costs + Construction Benefits Fee Paid + Fee Paid for Land Consolidation.

land value tax (土地價稅) (*TWN*) A property tax is levied once every year on the basis of the government announced land value. In terms of its computation, where the total value of all lands owned by any landowner does not exceed the initial point of land value subject to progressive rates, the land value tax is levied according to the basic rate of 1.5% of the government announced land value. Where the total value of all lands owned by any landowner exceeds the initial point of land value subject to progressive rates, the land value tax on that part of the total value which exceeds the said initial point is levied at different rates.

landed houses (*SGP*) A term used to refer to low rise dwelling houses usually not more than three storeys. It includes terrace, semi-detached bungalows/houses and bungalows/detached houses.

landing A flat platform at the top, bottom or in the middle of a flight of steps.

landlocked parcel A plot of land entirely surrounded by other privately owned lands.

landlord The owner of a property that has been leased.

landlord's improvements Any work of a capital nature, i.e., other than maintenance or repair, undertaken by the landlord, or by the tenant at the landlord's expense, which increases the value of the landlord's interest in a property.

landscape The setting of the land surrounding a building or structure. Nowadays, this is often done artificially to increase the value of the property.

landscape architect A person who plans and designs the decoration of the land surrounding a building or structure. This can be done by adding features such as water bodies, pavements, gardens, etc.

land-use planning certificate Document stating zoning and land-planning parameters.

land-use right certificate Document stating right to possess a specific plot of land for a stated period of time.

latent defect A hidden or concealed defect inherent in the design or construction of a building, which could not be discovered by inspection, despite reasonable care.

lateral support The right of a landowner to the natural support of his land by adjoining land. The adjoining owner has the duty not to change his land (such as lowering it) so as to cause this support to be weakened or removed.

layout Design, plan or arrangement of any given space, such as the rooms or apartment, etc.

lean-to A shed built against an adjoining the wall of another building, with three walls and a sloping roof.

leasable area Area by which rental is based on, usually equivalent to gross area.

lease A contract by which an owner of a property (known as lessor) gives the right of possession and use to another person (lessee), for a specified term and against a specified consideration.

lease agreement An agreement recording a lease between a lessor and a lessee.

lease restructure Whereby an existing lease is terminated / surrendered early and a new lease is signed on the same terms and conditions save for rent, incentives and term dates.

lease with option to purchase A lease agreement which gives the lessee the option of purchasing the property within or on or after a specified date. The price and conditions under which such purchase will take place are usually mentioned in the agreement.

leaseback An arrangement where a property is sold by a seller to a buyer and then leased to the former. Chronologically, the lease takes effect only after the sale, but it is considered part of the same transaction.

leasehold A property that is held under a lease. The title of the property remains with the owner who receives a lease rent which may be paid monthly, quarterly, annually or in lump sum for the entire period of the lease. The property reverts back to the owner after the period of the lease.

leasehold improvements Additions, alterations and improvements made to a leasehold property by the lessee.

leasehold value Total value of a leasehold right.

Leave & License (*IND*) An agreement recording a license between a licensor and licensee. The term of the license should not exceed 60 months. This kind of agreement is specific to Bombay (Mumbai) where corporates would enter into a Leave & License Agreement instead of a Lease Agreement to save on the Stamp duty and registration charges. A Leave & License agreement is usually for a period of 36 months.

legal description A description (of land, or any other thing) that is acceptable in a court of law.

legal owner A person or corporation or trust with a legal title over a property.

legal title Title recognized by law as the root of most other subordinate forms of title, e.g., lease or mortgage. However, legal title can be encumbered by a lease or mortgage, such that transfer of title will not affect the rights of those with other forms of interest over the property.

lemon A property that has considerably under performed on its proforma or has little likelihood to perform as expected.

lender An individual or corporate body which loans money that has to be repaid.

lessee The person or corporate body that takes a property on lease.

lessee improvements To enhance the demised premises for the tenants business operations, the tenant is entitled to carry out interior works with prior intimation to the landlord and subject to necessary approvals from the local authorities.

lessee's indemnification The lessee will indemnify the lessor/landlord against all and any loss or damage which the lessor/landlord may sustain by reason of claims brought against the lessor alleging bodily harm, injury and death to any person or damage to property which has been mutually discussed, described and agreed in the agreement.

lessor The person or body corporate that leases out a property.

lessor's indemnification The lessor/landlord will indemnify the lessee against all and any loss or damage which the lessee may sustain by reason of claims brought against the lessee alleging bodily harm, injury and death to any person or damage to property that has been mutually discussed, described and agreed in the agreement.

lettable area Floor area allocated to a unit or space and quoted for leasing purpose. The area is usually measured from the exterior of the enclosing walls of the units and includes the unit's share in the common area.

letter of comfort A letter from a third party to one of the parties to a contract giving an assurance that the recipient may expect the other party to, for example, honor some specified undertaking given in the contract, behave in a manner consistent with the understanding between the parties, be in a position to finance the deal or continue in existence as a subsidiary of the author. In property terms, in particular, such a letter may be written by a bank or other financial institution on behalf of a prospective developer, purchaser or lessee. The purpose is to give confidence to the recipient that the other party will have the resources to complete the contract or in other respects may be relied upon to act in accordance with what is promised. Whether such a letter will be legally binding as a distinct from giving the author a moral responsibility depends upon the circumstances of each case.

letter of intent A letter written by a party or joint venturer expressing an intention to proceed with the transaction in the future. A letter of intent is not usually legally binding.

letting Leasing or renting.

liability Debts and other obligations due to other parties.

license An official document giving a person or corporate body the permission to do something, such as enter, live in or use a property.

licensee A person who has a license.

lien The security provided when money is advanced against property.

life The time period during which a contract is valid.

life tenant A person whose lease rights are valid only during his or someone else's lifetime.

light and air easement A right restricting neighboring buildings from obstructing the flow of light and air. For example: the owner of a property may obtain light and air easement from his neighbor to ensure than his garden continues to get unrestricted sunlight at all times.

light industry Industries that do not cause pollution.

listing   83

light well A shaft that lights up and ventilates the inside rooms of a building.

limited recourse loan A lender who offers a limited recourse loan will in the event of the borrower defaulting only have recourse to property secured under the loan agreement and not to the unsecured property of the borrower.

line of credit A sum of money that is sanctioned by a bank or a lending institution for use by a borrower. Any amount up to the value of the sanctioned amount is then available on call for a given period of time.

lineal A measure of distance rather than a measure of area.

liquidated damages A pre-determined amount that has to be paid by a party who breaches a contract. The amount, or a method to arrive at the figure, is mentioned in the contract. Such amount has to be a close approximation of the losses incurred.

liquidation The sale of all financial assets to settle debts or claims following the closure of a business.

liquidity The state of having ready cash or easily encashable assets.

Listed Property Trust (LPT) (*AUS*) This term describes the securitized listed property sector in Australia, commonly referred to as REITs in other countries. It is one of the largest most sophisticated securitized property markets in the world and dominates the Australian investment landscape. They are essentially tax efficient vehicles where small and large investors can own a slice of an income producing real estate portfolio by buying and selling units (or shares) on the stock market. LPTs are traditionally passive low-risk structures but are increasingly offering investors higher returns through exposure to riskier activities such as development, land banking, accessing debt and other financial balance sheet engineering.

listing 1) The act of getting the shares of a company registered on a stock exchange, following which the general public can buy and sell such shares. 2) The listing or recording of a property that is for sale or lease.

litho sheet (*SGP*) A map published by the Survey Department from which plot dimensions can be ascertained.

littoral rights The rights of persons or countries with lands along the shores of oceans or lakes.

livability The minimum standards prescribed by governments for dwelling units.

loan The advance of a sum of money to another on the promise of repayment.

loan broker Someone who arranges a loan in return for a fee.

loan commitment An agreement to extend a loan on given terms.

loan package The sum total of all terms, conditions and information that go into a loan.

loan to value ratio (LVR) (*AUS*) Reflects the relationship between value and borrowings. Financial institutions use this to assess lending risk.

loan value Value of the property which is a certain percentage of its market value which the bank is willing to lend with only the property as security.

lobby Area just inside an apartment, building, hotel, theater or house that leads on to the more functional areas.

Local Environmental Plans (LEP) (*AUS*) Local Environmental Plans form the basis of all local authority planning schemes in Australia.

location Geographical position of a person or thing or structure. Good or bad locations depend on the intended use of the property.

lock-in period A period mentioned in the agreement during which neither party can terminate the agreement.

lodging The act of temporarily staying at a place, usually at a daily or weekly rental.

logistics A specialty within the supply chain process that plans, implements and controls the efficient flow and storage of goods, services and related information between the point of origin and point of consumption in order to meet customers' requirements.

long-term capital gain   Profit on the sale of an asset that has been held for a given period of time (usually more than one year; the period varies from country to country). Such profits are usually taxed at a rate lower than the highest rate of income tax.

long-term financing   An agreement for the advance of money for a long period of time. The legal definition of "long-term" varies from country to country.

long-term lease   A lease agreement that is valid for a long period of time. The legal definition of "long-term" varies from country to country.

loss of access   The taking away of the right to enter or exit a property.

lot   A portion or part of a property.

lot number (*SGP*)   Number identifying a property for legal purposes.

lump sum (building) contract   A contract placed with a builder at a fixed price.

luxury apartment   An apartment that has the top luxury facilities and amenities.

made-land/reclaimed A land artificially created by filling or dredging.

maintenance Periodic expenditure needed to preserve a property's original status rather than to improve that property. Activity required for compensating wear and tear.

maintenance fee Monthly assessment by association of owners and used for maintenance and repair of common areas. Usually a monthly fee paid.

major casualty The destruction of or damage by reasons beyond the control of either party to all or any part of the demised premises or the building and such destruction or damage cannot be rebuilt or repaired as reasonably determined by the architect.

make-good The act of returning a vacated facility back to its original state prior to the fit-out.

mal (*IDN*) Shopping center.

Malay Reserve Land (*MYS*) Land reserved for alienation to Malays or to natives of the State in which the land lies.

mall A public area-connecting individual stores in a shopping center. Modern malls are often enclosed, enabling all weather access. Also refers to an entire regional shopping center.

management 1) Person or persons responsible for managing a property or overseeing a job. 2) The act of managing, controlling or directing and carrying on a business.

management agreement A contract between the owner of a property and the party who agrees to manage it. Fees are based on a percentage of income but can be a flat incentive fee basis.

management corporation or MCST (*SGP*) A body corporate established under the Land Titles (Strata) Act which consists of all the owners of the units in a strata-titled development. The management corporation owns, controls and manages the common property.

marginal land Property that is barely profitable and which has poor income potential.

marina A small dock, for small yachts and cabin cruisers having supplies, and maintenance facilities.

market capitalization Number of shares issued by a listed entity multiplied by the unit price on the stock exchange.

market data approach Method of valuing a property through examination and comparison of recent sales of comparable properties.

market value Independently appraised value of real estate in a free competitive market. The highest price a buyer would pay and the lowest price a seller would accept, assuming that both were willing but not compelled to do so.

marketability The prospect of selling goods at a specific time, value and conditions.

marketable title Title that can be marketed or sold readily. Any court can enforce this title.

marriage value Latent value which is or would be released by the merger of two or more interests in land. For example, two adjoining parcels may be worth more as one property than the aggregate of their separate values. Similarly, two interests in the same property may have a greater value when merged than the sum of their individual values.

master lease A controlling lease in an apartment or office building that controls subleases.

master plan Document that describes, in narrative and with maps, an overall development concept including both present property uses as well as future land development plans. The plan may be prepared by a local government to guide private and public development or by a developer on a specific project.

Master Plan (*SGP*) The Master Plan translates the broad strategies proposed in the Concept Plan into detailed plans to guide the physical development of Singapore over the next 10 to 15 years. From the Master Plan, owners, architects, planners and developers know what can be built, where and how high the buildings can be, and how intensively the land can be used. The Master Plan is reviewed every five years with the latest coming in 2003. The set of 55 Development Guide Plans (DGPs) form the Master Plan for Singapore.

materai (*IDN*) Stamp duty.

mature land (熟地) (*CHN*) Land that has been developed for use and has utilities already installed, such as gas connections, electrical hook-up, water and sewage lines, etc.

maturity The due date when a mortgage or a loan must be paid.

median strip Strip of land that separates the lanes of opposing traffic.

merge To join with another. Mostly used to describe situations where two or more companies join together to form a larger entity. Usually, the identity of the smaller or the weaker company is absorbed by the larger or dominant one.

meter 1) A unit of length in the metric system that equals to 39.37 inches. 2) A measuring device used for measuring the usage of utilities, such as water, electricity, gas, etc.

metropolitan shopping center Largest type of establishment that has a concentration of one or more major department stores, a variety of retail stores, banks, restaurants and entertainment sections and has common parking and management. Also termed regional shopping center.

mezzanine Balcony or low ceiling overhang just above the main floor and below the next storey. In a theater, a mezzanine is the first balcony above the stage.

mezzanine loan A mezzanine loan is a relatively large, unsecured loan and normally not backed by a pledging of assets. The loan can carry a detachable warrant (the right to purchase a certain number of shares or stock or bonds at a given price for a period of time) or a similar mechanism to allow the lender to share in the future success of the business. Mezzanine loans are dependent on cash flow for repayment.

mineral rights Ownership rights to the minerals or other precious resources, in one's property. The privilege of gaining income from the sale of oil, gas, and other valuable resources found on land.

minimum lot The smallest lot area required or allowed for building under the municipal zoning code.

minimum rent A rent below which a variable rent will not fall, e.g., (i) a stated rent payable for the whole or part of the duration of a lease containing a formula for a possibly higher rent on review; (ii) a dead rent under a mining lease; and (iii) a base rent under a turnover lease.

mining lease A lease that, for a consideration, provides the lessee the right to mine minerals, such as gold, iron, coal, silver, etc., on the property of the lessor and sell the same.

misrepresentation An untrue statement. Misrepresentation is a form of fraud that could lead to cancellation of a contract and could lead to liabilities such as criminal and/or civil proceedings against the party who made such misrepresentations.

mixed use development Project which incorporates two or more property uses, for example, an office building with a retail offering on the lower levels.

month to month tenancy A tenancy when rent is being paid monthly and where the lease can be renewed for each succeeding month or terminated at the option of either party with sufficient notice.

monument A fixed object and point established by surveyors to determine land locations.

mortgage banker Company that uses its own money to provide loans and then usually sells them to investors such as insurance companies.

mortgage bond Bonds collateralized by real estate. Two kinds of mortgage bonds are senior mortgages, (having a first claim on assets and earnings), and junior mortgages (having a subordinate lien). A mortgage bond may have a closed-end provision that prevents the firm from issuing additional bonds of the same priority against the same property or may be an open-end mortgage that allows the issuance of additional bonds having equal status with the original issue.

mortgage broker An intermediary who sources mortgages for a fee.

mortgagee Financial institution that lends money to a borrower, taking a lien on that particular property as security.

mortgagee in possession (*AUS*) The position a lender takes in repossessing a property where the lender is in default of its loan obligations.

mortgagor Person or entity that borrows money to purchase a property, granting a mortgage on the property to the lender as security for the loan.

motel Originally a building on or near a major highway, providing food and accommodation to travelers with common parking for their vehicles. Now most motels offer most of the features of hotels, such as restaurants, recreation, etc.

mow (公畝) (*TWN*) It is a traditional measurement unit of area used in Taiwan. Its use is limited to real estate. 1 mow = 0.06667 hectare = 0.16473 acre.

mu (甬) (*CHN*) An area measurement unit in China, 15 mu = 1 hectare, 1 mu = 666.67 sq. m.

multi-family dwelling Residential property containing individual units for several households within the same structure. A building to house several families.

multiple agency The appointment of two or more agents to dispose of the same property independently of one another on the basis that only the successful agent is entitled to a commission.

multiple listing Arrangement where the real estate listings of many local agents are provided.

municipal-level industrial park Industrial zones that are sponsored locally at the provincial/municipal-level of government, prefecture-level and county-level.

Moving Annual Turnover (MAT) (*AUS*) This is a term used to analyze the performance of retail shopping centers and more specifically the running turnover (or consumer spend) levels reported by retailers in major shopping centers.

negative amortization A loan repayment schedule in which the outstanding principal balance of the loan increases, rather than amortizing, because the scheduled monthly payments do not cover the full amount required to amortize the loan. The unpaid interest is added to the outstanding principal, to be repaid later.

negative cash flow A situation where income is less than expenses.

negative gearing (AUS) It is a financial tool utilized by Australian investors whereby the cost of borrowing less the income received can be offset against taxable income from other investment sources. This makes property an attractive investment asset class.

negotiable Capable of being negotiated; transferable by assignment or endorsement to another person; as a negotiable note or bill of exchange.

negotiable instrument A promise to pay money, transferable from one person to another. A bill of exchange, check, promissory note, or other written contract for payment that may serve as a substitute for money. It is simple in form and easy to transfer.

negotiation The deliberation which takes place between the parties prior to an agreement. That which transpires in the negotiation makes no part of the agreement, unless introduced into it.

neighborhood shopping center A concentration of retail, service, and entertainment enterprises designed to serve the surrounding region (neighborhood) and having a common parking lot.

negligence The omission to do something which a reasonable person would ordinarily do under the circumstances, or doing something which a reasonable person would ordinarily not do under the circumstances. The failure to take reasonable care given the circumstances.

net absorption Change in occupied real estate stock between two points in time.

net effective rate The rent after allowing rent-free periods, rebates, incentives or concessions, if any.

net floor area Refers to the useable floor area in a building. For example the net floor area of an office floor is the gross floor area less areas occupied by columns, walls, common passageways, lift lobbies and toilets.

net internal area (NIA) (Formerly sometimes referred to as "effective floor area.") The usable space within a building measured to the internal finish of structural, external or party walls, but excluding toilets, lift and plant rooms, stairs and lift-wells, common entrance halls, lobbies and corridors, internal structural walls and car-parking areas.

net present value method (NPV) A method used in discounted cash flow analysis to find the sum of money representing the difference between the present value of all inflows and all outflows of cash associated with the project by discounting each at a target yield.

net rent The stated rental on a net floor area basis, exclusive of outgoings.

net rentable area The actual area for which rent can be charged.

nilai buku (*IDN*) Book value.

non-performing loan A bank loan where the borrower has both ceased to make full interest payments, such that the lender has stopped earning interest and one where the borrower is likely to default on the principal.

nonbearing wall A wall that does not provide any support to the structure in which it is located or the floors above it. It carries only its own weight and is used to separate an area.

nonconforming use Property use, violating the current zoning ordinance.

nonexclusive listing A listing given to a number of brokers without legal responsibility to compensate any except the one who first gets hold of a buyer who is ready, willing and able to meet the terms of the listing or secures the seller's acceptance.

non-freehold estate Property that is not owned by the occupant but is held under lease or license.

non-landed properties (*SGP*) This refers to condominiums and apartment housing.

nonrecourse loan A type of loan where the lenders may take the property pledged as collateral to satisfy a debt but have no ability to take the other assets of the borrower.

normal wear and tear Deterioration or decline in the value of a property due to use, physical damage, old age or environmental factors.

notice to quit A certain and reasonable notice required by law, custom, special agreement or statute, enabling either the landlord or the tenant or the assignees or representatives of either of them, without the consent of the other, to determine a tenancy from year to year or other periodic tenancy.

notices A legal notification required by law or agreement or imparted by operation of law as a result of some fact.

novation Substitution of another borrower in place of the original borrower or lessee, releasing the latter from all obligations. This is done with the consent of the lender or landlord.

NRI (*IND*) Non-resident Indian. This refers to an Indian who is a citizen and resident of other countries. Non-resident Indians often return to India on periodic visits because of family or business ties and are known to bring investments, skills and spending power which helps to foster India's economic development.

nuisance A land use incompatible with surrounding land uses. Any activity by a property owner that annoys or seriously disturbs the neighborhood making it difficult for other property owners to use or enjoy their own property.

null and void That which cannot be legally enforced or is not legally binding.

NZIV (*NZL*) New Zealand Institute of Valuers.

NZPI (*NZL*) New Zealand Property Institute.

obsolescence A loss in the utility of an asset due to the development of improved or superior equipment, but not due to physical deterioration.

occupancy Occupancy rates represent rooms nights occupied expressed as a percentage of room nights available, during any given period. For other properties (other than a hotel), it is the measure of the percentage of floor space occupied by tenants as compared to the total lettable area of the building.

Occupancy Certificate (OC) A document issued by the local municipal authority building proposal department that provides no objection to occupy the building under reference for its specified use. The OC is issued only once the building has been completed in all respects and can be occupied. A corporate can carry out its commercial activity only once the premises/building has received its OC.

occupancy cost Cost faced by a tenant associated with the occupancy of premises. This includes charges such as rent, taxes, rates and insurance.

occupation permit (入伙紙) (*HKG*) A permit issued by the Building Authority to certify that a building (the construction of which is governed by the Building Ordinance) can be occupied.

occupied stock Total amount of stock which is leased or owner occupied.

offer An expression of willingness to purchase or sell a property at a specified price; presenting for acceptance a price for a property parcel; the bid price in a real estate or security transaction.

offer and acceptance These two requirements of a contract signifying mutual consent combined with valuable consideration are the major elements of a binding contract.

offeree An entity that receives an offer.

offeror An entity that makes an offer.

office A room, set of rooms, or building where the business such as paper work, administration, clerical services, and consultation with clients and associates of a commercial or industrial organization or of a professional person is conducted.

off-site Improvements or activities taking place away from the site or located away from the site.

off-site improvements Development of land adjacent to the property to make it habitable such as side-walks, paved access road, sewers, etc.

on-site improvements Directly enhancing the physical nature of the property such as renovating a building, installing a new driveway and parking lot and gardening.

open book Where a contractor is required to provide and verify to the client the actual cost of the works carried out by others (normally associated with construction management).

open house A term referring to a house that is left open for prospective buyers to see or inspect. This normally does not involve a formal appointment as the time and days when the house remains open is specified or fixed.

open listing An agreement permitting a real estate agent to sell the property while also allowing the homeowner or other agents to attempt to make the sale.

open market value The amount that a seller may expect to obtain for property, services, or securities in the open market.

open-end mortgage A mortgage or trust deed in which the amount borrowable can be increased by the mortgagor, that is, the mortgagee may secure additional money from the mortgagee (lender) through an agreement which typically stipulates a maximum amount that can be borrowed.

openable wall An openable wall often used between meeting rooms that can be moved to one side to create a larger space.

operating expenses Expenses incurred in managing an investment property, including repairs and maintenance, legal and management fees.

option The right to buy or sell an item at a specified price within a given period of time. The right, if not exercised after a specified time, expires. For example, a lease of a property with the option to buy.

oral contract The term refers to a verbal contract made between parties where there is partial or no written agreement. These types of contracts have a very weak legal standing and are dependent on witnesses to the said contract.

ordinance A statute enacted by a city or town especially enactments of the legislative body of a municipal corporation or a county.

ordinary asset Property which includes inventory for sale, or property used in connection with trade, business, or source of income.

ordinary repairs Minor day-to-day repair and maintenance of a property to prevent wear and tear.

outgoings Costs incurred by the owner of an interest in property, usually calculated on a yearly basis, e.g., management, repairs, rates, insurance and rent payable to the holder of a superior interest, as appropriate to his contractual or other liabilities. It is prudent to make annual provision for future items involving expenditure at intervals of more than one year.

Outline Zoning Plan (分區計劃大綱圖) (*HKG*) Statutory plans prepared under the Town Planning Ordinance which depicts the land use zoning.

overage income Rental based on a percentage of sales or profit that is over and above the constant rental amount.

overbook To accept reservations in excess of the number that can be accommodated.

overhead Fixed or indirect expenses of a business or property. Overhead includes items such as salaries, office rent, and other such administrative and marketing costs.

overseas Chinese（海外华人）(*CHN*) People of Chinese ethnicity whose primary nationality is not Chinese. That is, they are residents and citizens of other countries. Overseas Chinese have been known to be significant economic driving forces for several countries in South East Asia. With the opening up of China to foreign investments, overseas Chinese from Hong Kong, Taiwan, Singapore and Thailand are known to bring their investments, skills and spending power into China, fuelling its economic development.

owner An entity possessing ownership rights to a property.

owner occupied A property that is occupied by an entity that possesses ownership rights to the said property.

parking ratio The relationship between the number of car parking spaces and the amount of accommodation available for other uses within a building or group of buildings.

parkway A broad landscaped highway, often divided by a planted median strip.

Part Occupation Certificate (OC) A document issued by the building proposal department of the local municipal authority that provides a no objection to occupy the specific floor in the building under reference for its specified use. The Part OC is issued only once the premises/building has been completed in all respects and can be occupied. A corporate can occupy and carry on its operations only once the demised premises has received its OC.

partition An internal wall normally constructed from light weight dry materials such as metal or timber framework with plasterboard sheet lining.

party wall A wall that separates two or more properties on the same parcel of land under different ownership.

pa-si-bum-rung-thong-thi (*THA*) Local development tax. This tax only applies to land. The tax rate varies greatly, depending on the location and assessed value of the land. Typically, it ranges from baht 0.5 to baht 400 per rai (1,600 sq. m.) (2005).

pa-si-mul-la-ka-perm (*THA*) Value-added tax (VAT), which is a consumption tax based on the value of goods and services offered by traders, businesses or persons in Thailand. It is calculated from the price of the goods and services. The standard rate is 7% (2005).

pa-si-rong-ruen (*THA*) House and land tax. This is a tax on assessed rental income and only applies to properties that are rented out. Rental contracts are typically split into three components that are taxed separately as follows: 1) rental: subject to a house and land tax of 12.5% of annual rental receipts; 2) lease of furniture: subject to a 7% VAT; and 3) service charge: subject to a 7% VAT (2005).

passing rent The amount of rent as at current date or the date of valuation.

patent defect Visible defect in a product, property or document. In legal matters, the term refers to a defect, which cannot be corrected on the document itself, and a fresh document rectifying the flaw has to be obtained.

patio An area adjoining the house that is paved with concrete, flagstone, brick, etc. and is used for relaxation or recreation purposes.

PBB (Pajak Bumi Bangunan) (*IDN*) Real estate tax.

PCA (*AUS*) Property Council of Australia (peak industry lobby group).

PCNZ (*NZL*) Property Council of New Zealand.

PCNZ: Guide for Measurement of Rentable Areas (*NZL*) A formula for the measurement of rentable areas, devised by the Property Council of New Zealand and generally accepted as the methodology to be applied in the country.

pedestrian overpass Bridge constructed over a highway, railway, roads, etc., for the use of pedestrians.

Pejabat Pembuat Akte Tanah (PPAT) (*IDN*) Generally notaries who are authorized to produce land deeds.

penal rent A financial punishment of a tenant for failing to honor his obligation to pay rent at the proper time, taking the form of a vastly higher figure being payable during the period of default.

Pengikatan Perjantian Jual Beli (PPJB) (*IDN*) Sale and purchase binding agreement for a real estate transaction.

penilaian (*IDN*) Appraisal.

penthouse A luxury dwelling unit located on the top floor or roof of a high-rise building.

per annum By the year. On a yearly basis. For each year.

per capita A Latin term that translates into "by head," per unit of population; per person. In legal terms it means equally to each individual. Per capita distribution of an estate provides each descendant with an equal share of the estate's assets regardless of the degree of his or her kinship. Children, grandchildren, great-grandchildren, etc., all receive equal shares.

per diem Per day or daily.

percentage lease (turnover rent) A lease of property in which the rental is based on a percentage of the volume of sales made upon the leased premises. It usually stipulates a minimum rental and is regularly used for retailers who are tenants. Usually does not fall below a base rent.

performance bond A bond, given by a contractor and issued by an insurance company to guarantee the completion of contracted work.

perimeter The boundary lines of a property expressed in terms of measurement in length.

perkantoran (*IDN*) Office building.

permitted use A use allowed by the deemed grant of planning permission under the local development control norms.

perpetuity The condition of being never ending. In legal terms it refers to an interest under which property is less than completely alienable for longer than the law allows.

personal property Property of an entity that is not termed by law as real property.

perumahan (*IDN*) Residential estate.

phang-muang (*THA*) Town plan.

phoenix company (*NZL*) A company that goes into voluntary liquidation to avoid litigation then re-emerges essentially as the same company, but under a different name.

physical depreciation Decline in value of property due to physical damage to the property such as wear and tear or lack of maintenance.

pile Perpendicular support piece of a structure, driven into the ground, which supports the foundation.

pillar A long, slender, perpendicular structure used as a support.

ping (坪) (*TWN*) It is a traditional measurement unit of area used in Taiwan. Its use is limited to real estate. 1 ping = 3.305 square meters = 36 square feet.

pingfang (平房) (*CHN*) Chinese bungalow, which is an older type of housing accommodation in China, with one storey and usually of poor quality.

pitch Slope of a roof. Pitch is the ratio of vertical rise to horizontal run.

planned (unit) development Residential project that features dense clusters of houses surrounded by areas of open space, owned in common and maintained by a nonprofit association.

planning commission Governmental body having the responsibility for planning the future development of a jurisdictional area. A planning commission is responsible for developing and managing a zoning ordinance as well as interfacing with a professional planning department.

planning region (*SGP*) Singapore is divided into five planning regions to facilitate the planning of the use and development of land for the whole of Singapore. The five regions are Central Region, East Region, North East Region, North Region and West Region.

plans Drawings (made to scale) which are required for a construction project and includes the subcontractors drawings also.

plat (plat map) A map of a parcel of land showing the boundaries of individual properties that has been divided into lots.

plat book Public record of maps showing the division of streets, blocks and lots and providing the measurements of the individual parcels.

pledge The pawning of property as a security against a loan.

pledged account loan A savings bank account that is used as a collateral security against a loan.

pledgee Entity to whom a mortgage or property is pledged.

pledgor Entity who is responsible for making the payments on a mortgage on property that has been pledged.

plot 1) An area of land that is used for a specific purpose such as a cemetery plot. 2) The term may refer to a piece of land on which a structure or improvements are to be built.

plot plan Plan represented in the form of a scale diagram that shows the proposed or existing use of a specific parcel of land such as the location of the structures within the boundaries of the property, utility services, compass directions, etc.

plot ratio Plot ratio determines the maximum gross floor area (GFA) allowable on a plot of land. A plot ratio of two means that the GFA allowable is two times the site's area.

plottage The acquisition of several smaller contiguous lands to make a larger, more useful and valuable property or for putting the same to specific use.

plottage increment A term that refers to the increase in the value of land by plottage.

plumbing The system of pipes and other apparatus for conveying water, liquid wastes, etc., as in a building.

PMI Private Mortgage Insurance.

PMI pass-through certificates Conventional mortgage securities that are supported by mortgages that are insured by private mortgage insurance companies.

PML (probable maximum loss) (*JPN*) An index used to assess the risk of possible damage a structure may incur in the event of a natural disaster, more specifically an earthquake. It is included in the engineering report in the due diligence procedure and the lower the number, the more earthquake-tolerant the structure.

point A term referring to one hundredth of a loan amount. Different from a basis point which is one hundredth of one per cent.

point letter Letter issued by a lender guaranteeing a specified number of points on a loan for a given period of time.

policy A term used to describe all insurance contracts.

portfolio A collection of property or other investments held in one ownership.

possession Actual or physical holding or occupancy of a property with or without rightful ownership.

possibility of reverter Legal term to describe a situation where a person having relinquished his right (by sale, gift, etc.) over a property, retains the right to reassert his claims over it if the property is not used for the purpose for which it was sold, gifted, etc. Example: A person sells a property on condition that it will be used for an orphanage. If it is used for any other purpose the seller has the right to demand a reversal of the original transaction.

post To display (an announcement) in a place of public view or to cover (a wall, for example) with posters, notices, etc.

postdated Incorporating a later date on an instrument such as a check or a deed than the date on which it was signed.

potable Any liquid especially water that is fit for drinking.

power center A form of specialty store which merchandises the widest range of merchandise of a particular kind. For example, Home Depot is a power center for Do-It-Yourself (DIY) home improvement merchandise.

power of attorney A legal instrument authorizing one to act as another's attorney or agent.

power of sale A power granted (as in a will, trust, or mortgage) to sell the property to which the power relates often under specified circumstances (as upon the default of a mortgage).

PR Public relations / permanent resident.

practical completion When a facility is completed to a stage where it is fit for occupation (minor defects may remain at this time).

pre-commitment Space directly pre-leased in buildings prior to their completion or refurbishment.

pre-emption right The right of first refusal or to make an offer before others.

prefabricated house A modular structure built of blocks manufactured elsewhere and assembled at the site.

prefabrication A technique whereby large units of a building or a part of it are produced in factories to be assembled, ready-made, on the building site.

preliminary title report A report filed by a lawyer who has conducted a preliminary search of a property's title. Preliminary title reports are followed by final title reports that may confirm the findings of the earlier report or provide data on additional facts which come to light following a more detailed search.

premises 1) The preliminary or explanatory statements or facts of a document, as in a deed. 2) Land and the buildings on it.

premium 1) A sum of money or bonus paid in addition to a regular price, salary, or other amount. 2) The amount paid, often in addition to the interest, to obtain a loan. 3) The amount paid or payable, often in installments, for an insurance policy. 4) The amount at which something is valued above its par or nominal value, as money or securities. 5) The amount at which a securities option is bought or sold.

premium rent 1) A rent above the level which a property could reasonably be expected to command in the open market on normal terms. Such rents may be justified in instances where the tenant receives a present or future benefit against the market, e.g., in inflationary conditions where upward-only rent reviews are normally required at five-yearly intervals, the tenant may be prepared to pay a higher rent if fixed for a longer period of, say, 10 years. 2) A rent which is higher than would reasonably be expected because the tenant is particularly anxious to secure the property.

prepaid interest Interest paid before it is due.

prepaid items Advance payment of expenses such as taxes, insurance, rent, etc., on a property that may be prorated upon sale of the said property.

prepayment The payment of a debt or obligation, in part or full prior to its due date. Such payment may or may not result in penalties, depending on the terms of the contract.

pre-sale Similar to buying off plan, in which buyer purchases part of a future development. It is commonly used by developers to finance projects.

present value The future worth of a property or a sum of money discounted to its present-day equivalent, taking account of all relevant circumstances, including for example, inflation.

price 1) The amount as of money or goods, asked for or given in exchange for something else. 2) The cost at which something is obtained.

price-earnings ratio The comparison of the market price of a share of stock to the earning per share of that stock, expressed as a ratio. Also called the P/E ratio.

prime Refers to property which is the best in terms of rentals, location, etc.

prime tenant The key tenant necessary to obtain construction financing. The tenant may be deemed "prime" because of its financial strength, rather than by the amount of space it occupies.

prime yield Descriptive of the current yield used in the valuation of property let at full market value and which — for the class of property concerned — is of the best physical quality, in the best location, and with the best tenant's covenant and contemporary lease terms.

principal Borrowed amount of money minus any payments subsequently made (does not include the interest component). Alternately, the term refers to an entity giving authority to an attorney or an agent.

principal contractor The contractor responsible for the site and all activities that are carried out on it whilst under construction (has a major implication regarding safety).

priority clause A clause in a loan agreement that acknowledges that a prior loan enjoys first charge over a mortgaged asset.

private land grant The transfer of land owned by the government to a private party. Such transfer may be in lieu of money or for charitable or other purposes.

private property Property owned by a private individual, company, corporation or a non-government body.

private treaty The most common method of disposal of real property, in which negotiations are carried out between the vendor and prospective purchasers (or their respective agents) privately and in comparative secrecy, normally without any limit on the time within which they must be completed before contracts are exchanged.

professional negligence A term often applied to the failure to meet the higher standard of care owed by "professional" advisers or other skilled persons to their clients or third parties by virtue of the special skill and experience which they hold themselves out to possess. Such is not strictly a special branch of the law of negligence but demonstrates that the standard of care — and thus the question whether there has been negligence — will depend upon circumstances of the particular case, including the knowledge, skill and experience of the person concerned.

profit Excess of income over expenses in a business transaction. Gain.

profits method Method of valuation through which the valuer looks at the operating costs of the business and assesses the amount of rent that the occupier can afford by way of rent. It is generally used where there is some degree of monopoly attached to the property.

program (schedule) A group of activities set out in sequence to provide a plan of how a project will be executed.

project A piece of planned work or an activity which is completed over a period of time and intended to achieve a particular aim, normally the construction of a facility.

Project Information Memorandum (PIM) (*NZL*) A report issued by the local council prior to issuing a building consent, confirming that building work may proceed, subject to any of the requirements under legislation.

project management The process of planning, organizing, staffing, directing and controlling a project.

property The right and interest in lands and chattels to the exclusion of others. Something owned; any tangible or intangible possession that is owned by someone.

property asset management A comprehensive form of management, similar to property portfolio management except that the managers have a wider degree of discretion. The primary objective is to maximize overall financial performance.

property brief An abridged or concise description of the property for sale, issued by the seller and approved by the seller and given to the buyer.

property investment trust A financial organization on the lines of a mutual fund that collects money from a large body of investors and deploys the same in properties. It derives its income stream from rental and from the sale of properties that appreciate above their purchase price.

property line Official dividing line between two properties. Legal boundary of property.

property management The range of functions concerned with looking after a building, including collection of rents, payment of outgoings, maintenance including repair, provision of services, insurance and supervision of staff employed for services, together with negotiations with tenants or prospective tenants. The extent of and responsibility for management between landlord and tenant depend on the terms of the lease(s). The landlord may delegate some or all of these functions to managing agents.

property management agreement An agreement between an owner of a property and the manager hired to manage the same. The agreement lays down in detail the scope of activities entailed in the service along with the terms and conditions of payment for the services rendered.

Property Operation, Maintenance and Energy Costs (POMEC) All expenses incurred by the owner of a property, usually a hotel, resort, commercial property or shopping mall, on maintaining and running the property. Includes expenses incurred on electricity, gas and fuels. The term originated in the hospitality industry, but is now used across almost all types of properties.

property portfolio management The unified management of a group of properties which are held in one ownership. Decisions taken in respect of any issue are reached on the basis of achieving the maximum benefit for the owners, having regard to the effect on the portfolio as a whole rather than on an individual property.

property sector Classification of property assets by type, including office, retail, residential, industrial and hotel.

property tax The tax on property ownership levied by the government or local authority. Also known as real estate tax.

property tenure (*SGP*) The time period (usually in years) over which the owner of the property or land enjoys the legal right of use subject to other restrictive covenants that may or may not be in place. Most properties are either freehold, 999-year or 99-year in tenure.

proprietor (*MYS*) Any person or body for the time being registered as the proprietor of any alienated land.

proprietorship The state of being proprietor. The ownership of a business by an individual as against a partnership or corporation.

prospect A potential customer, client, or purchaser.

provisional permission (PP) (*SGP*) This refers to the conditional approval granted by the Minister for National Development or the competent authority to develop any land subject to conditions in accordance with the development rules in force.

PTUN (*IDN*) Administrative court.

public housing Housing units built by government or statutory boards, which are sold or rented to individuals and families, usually from lower income groups at subsidized sale prices or low rental rates.

public land Acreage held by the government for conservation purposes. Public lands are generally undeveloped, with limited activities such as grazing, wildlife management, recreation, timbering, mineral development, water development and hunting.

public tender (open tender) A tender open to any member of the public who is able to fulfill the requirements specified in the tender document, the tender being advertised for this purpose.

purchase agreement A contract documenting the terms and conditions which govern the purchase of a property.

purchase and leaseback A purchase of a property and subsequent lease from the buyer back to the seller. Although the lease actually follows the sale, both are agreed to as part of the same transaction.

put option (*AUS*) A legal document requiring the purchaser to acquire an interest in property if activated by the vendor.

pyung (*KOR*) It is a traditional standard measurement unit of area used in Korea. Its use is limited to real estate. 1 pyung = 3.3058 sq. m. = 35.58 sq. ft.

quality The quality of a building is dependent upon several factors including 1) the market image/prestige of the building; 2) the quality of services including air conditioning, security, speed of lifts and amenities; 3) the views/outlook of the building; 4) layout: the floor size and its flexibility; 5) level of parking provided; 6) quality of construction and finishes; and 7) standard of maintenance.

quantity survey method Estimated itemization of all costs in constructing a structure including site acquisition and preparation and a detailed cost estimate of all materials, labor and overhead required to reproduce a structure. Contractors in preparing a project's bid price use quantity surveys. Also, an appraisal estimate of the replacement cost of a structure including current costs of materials and labor.

quantum allowance In a valuation of a relatively large property when appropriate in market terms, an end deduction from the rental or capital value, which has been calculated by reference to comparable smaller properties; its purpose is to reflect the greater size of the subject of the valuation.

quit rent (*MYS*) Land tax levied on property owners, which varies from one state to another, payable to the land office. The rate for quit rent also varies with land category and size.

rack rate The rate a lodging establishment charges for a room before any discount has been taken into account. It is the published rate for a guest room. A rack rate is often the rate a lodging establishment would offer a guest if he / she approaches the establishment directly.

ra-ka-pra-mern-raj-ja-karn (*THA*) Official assessed value.

range Land used for grazing livestock. In some countries, it also means an administrative sub-division.

ratable estate Property on which tax is levied.

ratchet clause A mechanism in a lease agreement which prevents the rental payable from decreasing at a rent review.

rate index Benchmark or index on which the interest rate of a floating rate loan is based.

rate of occupancy The percentage of all rental units (i.e., hotel guest rooms) are occupied or rented at a given time expressed as a percentage.

rate of return The annual percentage return from an investment.

rateable value An estimate of its annual open market rental value at a designated valuation reference date made on the assumption that the property was then vacant and to let.

raw land Term for land that does not have facilities or services such as water, traffic, electricity, communication infrastructure or gas. Virgin land.

raze Knock down.

real estate Of or relating to land and property.

real estate broker A person who brings buyers and sellers or lessors and lessees or tenants and landlords together and receives a percentage of the deal value as compensation.

Real Estate Developers Association of Singapore (REDAS) (*SGP*) REDAS comprises of members from all key property developers/players of Singapore and is active in making representations to all bodies, public or semi-public in nature, that concern the planning, organization, promotion, development, financing and administration of real estate development.

real estate license A license issued by a competent authority for carrying on the business of a real estate broker or developer.

realty Same as real estate.

recision of a contract The abrogation of an agreement.

recital Explanation of facts in a deed or agreement.

reclamation The process of increasing the value of land by improving (usually) wasteland or swampland and making it economically useful.

reconditioning Renovation.

reconveyance The transfers of title to a mortgaged property from a trustee to the equitable owner after all sums due plus interest have been repaid.

rectification of boundaries The correction or adjustment of the line(s) separating two properties in order to correctly reflect the title of lands.

reddendum Legal term for an owner retaining some rights in a sale or lease deed.

redemption The act of paying off amounts due on mortgaged properties following which the owner's unencumbered title to a property is restored.

redevelopment The improvement of land in terms of an urban development plan.

re-entry The right to retake possession of a property that has been given to another party by way of mortgage, lease, rental, etc. Legal action is often necessary to enforce this right.

refurbishment The act of renovating or upgrading an existing property, either internally or externally.

regional shopping center See metropolitan shopping center.

regional shopping centre (*AUS*) An enclosed shopping mall anchored by at least two department stores, two discount department stores and two supermarkets.

registered agreement (*IND*) A Leave & License Agreement/Lease Agreement which has been adequately stamped with the applicable stamp duty and then registered with the sub-registrar.

registration (*IND*) Every Leave & License Agreement/Lease Agreement in India has to be registered with the office of the sub-registrar of assurances (local authority) for it to be enforceable by law. This is the obligation of the licensor/lessor/landlord. However, the cost towards registration of the agreement is usually paid by the licensee/lessee.

reinstatement 1) Payments that restore a contract from default and make it live once more. 2) The act of putting a part or the whole of a building or structure back into the condition which existed at some relevant previous date.

REINZ (*NZL*) Real Estate Institute of New Zealand.

REIT (real estate investment trust) A REIT is a corporation or trust that uses the pooled capital of many investors to purchase and manage real estate assets and / or mortgage loans. REITs are traded on major stock exchanges like normal stocks. They are often also granted special tax considerations. Key benefits of REITs are their inherent liquidity and their instant pricing. REITs enable investment in all major asset types including shopping centers and other commercial or industrial properties.

relocation Refers to the process of relocating people living on a future development site to another area.

remise To give up a claim.

remnant Non-acquired portion of a larger property that has been taken over by the government in eminent domain proceedings, such that this remaining portion is practically of no value.

remodeling The improvement of a structure by changing its plans or functions.

rendering The drawing of a plan or sketch of a building.

renegotiation The act of trying to impose new terms on an existing agreement. Some agreements specifically allow the renegotiation of certain terms like rents or rate of interest after given intervals.

renewal An agreement to continue an existing contract on similar or slightly modified terms at the end of the previous term.

renewal option A clause in an agreement that gives either or both parties the right but not the obligation.

renewal term Upon the conclusion of the initial term as mentioned in the agreement, the lessee at its option may renew the agreement for an additional period (usually three to five years) which is described in the agreement as the renewal term.

renovated property (装修房) (*CHN*) Apartments in China that are fully finished and fitted out with wardrobes, bathroom fittings, cabinets and floor finishes. Typically targeted at middle and high-income families in major cities such as Beijing, Shanghai, Guangzhou, Shenzhen but are also being introduced into fast-growing cities such as Suzhou and Hangzhou by foreign developers as they raise the standard of residential developments in these cities.

renovation Same as reconditioning.

rent controls Laws in some countries that set upper limits on the amount of rents that can be charged by landlords.

rent free period Period during which the landlord does not charge rents from the lessee. This is usually at the beginning of the contract period when the lessee needs time to furnish the property to make it fit for use.

rent review A provision in a lease whereby the amount of the rent is to be reconsidered at stated intervals, e.g., every three or five years, or on specified dates. The method and procedure for reviewing the rent are outlined in the lease. Failing agreement between the parties, there is normally provision for reference to a third party, i.e., an arbitrator or independent expert.

rent subsidy Subsidy that some governments pay for renting properties to special or disadvantaged groups. In some countries, this also means a rebate on taxes levied on rental income of landlords to enable them to carry out essential repairs to a property.

rentable area The area in square feet or square meters that a landlord can charge rent for.

rental A periodic payment for the use of land or property made by a tenant to a landlord under a lease or tenancy agreement. Rent is therefore both a charge on occupation and also a return to owners of property.

rental agent A real estate broker who helps a landlord to find a tenant, in return for a consideration, usually a percentage of the annual or monthly rent.

rental agreement An agreement between a landlord and a tenant setting forth the terms of a lease.

rental commencement Refers to the date when the lessee's obligation to pay rent commences.

rental review At the end of the initial term of the agreement, the rental review comes into place based on the then market conditions. Rental review is usually pre-determined and the increase is capped at the time of execution of the initial term of the agreement.

rental value The market rent of a property.

repairs The replacement of broken or damaged portions of a property.

replacement The substitution of a broken or damaged portion of a property with a similar item.

replacement cost The cost of a similar or identical property.

replacement value The cost of replacing damaged items with new items. It will often be greater than the value of the original items before damage occurred. In the case of valuable antiques, replacement may be impracticable regardless of cost.

resale flat (*SGP*) A Housing & Development Board (HDB) flat available on the open resale market, as opposed to direct first time flat purchases from HDB.

resale levy (*SGP*) This is the sum of money that a seller needs to pay if he intends to buy.

rescind To cancel a contract.

reservation A right that has been retained by an original owner of land. Also refers to land that has been set aside by the government for a particular purpose or group of people.

reserve The setting aside of funds for any purpose. Such purpose may or may not be specified, e.g., reserve for renewal of fixtures fittings and equipment.

reserve list (government land sales program) (*SGP*) A Government Land Sales site in the Reserve List will only be offered for sale via a land tender bid process if there is at least one successful application from an interested developer who is able to offer a minimum land price for the site in question that is acceptable to the government. This Government Reserve Price is usually determined by the Chief Assessor of Singapore. The successful applicant must undertake to subsequently submit a bid for the land in the tender at or above the minimum price offered by him in the application.

reserved land (*MYS*) Land reserved for a public purpose for the time being.

reservoir A designated area where water is stored.

residence Dwelling place.

residential building A building in which people live.

residual method (residual valuation) A method of determining the value of a property which has potential for development, redevelopment or refurbishment. The estimated total cost of the work, including fees and other associated expenditure, plus an allowance for interest, developer's risk and profit, is deducted from the gross value of the completed project. The resultant figure is then adjusted back to the date of valuation.

residuary estate The property of a deceased that remains after all taxes and bequests have been met.

resort hotel A full-service lodging establishment located in a place frequented by people for relaxation or recreation.

resort property Property that people visit on vacations or weekends for fun and relaxation.

resource consent (*NZL*) A land use consent, issued under the Resource Management Act, by a local council.

restoration The carrying out of repairs to a building in order to make it appear as it did originally.

restriction in interest (*MYS*) Means a limitation imposed by the state authority on any of the powers conferred on a proprietor of land, normally on the use of the land.

retained earnings The total profit or loss of the company less the total of all dividends paid, since the company's startup.

retaining wall Wall that restrains water or soil from flowing into an inappropriate area.

retention An agreed sum held from the contractors payments until completion in case of non performance of the contractor.

retrofitting The extensive renovation to a building often involving major changes to its layout, services and structure, to enhance its functionality and update or improve its appeal and marketability with a view to achieve better investment returns and capital appreciation.

return for risk and profit A percentage of costs to allow for the developer's annual risk and profit in a valuation to determine a ground rent by deductions from actual or estimated occupation rent(s).

return on equity (ROE) Net income for the period expressed as percentage of average shareholders' equity for the period.

revaluation Same as reassessment.

reversion The right to reclaim title to a property at the end of a temporary estate.

revenue per available room (RevPAR) The product of average daily rate (ADR) and average occupancy.

reversionary yield The percentage return on today's price or value that will be derived when the current market rents become payable. This yield relates the future growth in net income to the historic cost or value of the property.

right of first refusal A right given by one party to another whereby the first party is obliged to give the second party a chance to acquire an asset before he offers it to anyone else.

right of last refusal A right given by one party to another whereby the first party is obliged to give the second party the last chance to bid on a property.

right of survivorship The right of a survivor to the property of a deceased person. Usually found in lease or rental agreements.

right of way The right to pass over land not legally or specifically belonging to the user.

rise The height of a slope.

risk averse In real estate, generally refers to an investor's aversion to volatile returns.

risk management The identification, assessment and management of issues that may cause an adverse effect on the project or the stakeholders.

ROFR (*IND*) Right of first refusal is provided by the lessor to the lessee on an additional area which has not been committed by the lessee. The lessor on finding another interested tenant for the area will provide the lessee with an opportunity to take up the area within a specified number of days, if the lessee does not take up the area within the specified number of days, the lessor will go ahead with the interested tenant.

rolling refurbishment The staged upgrading of premises which avoids the complete removal of tenants but which does not result in a substantial upgrade of a building's fabric and services.

room count The number of rooms in a building or apartment.

room nights available (RNA) The number of guest rooms/units multiplied by the number of days for which they were available during any given period.

root of title Document that establishes beyond dispute the title of an unregistered land. It traces the title to the property back in time, sometimes up to a hundred years or more, and from that point to the present, leaving no scope for any dispute over the right and title of the current owner.

rosenka (*JPN*) Refers to the prices of land at selected sample spots on major streets in the country issued by the National Tax Agency. It is used to assess inheritance and gift taxes and is normally assumed at 80% of the value (koji-chika) issued by the Ministry of Land, Infrastructure and Transport.

row houses Residential houses within a housing estate having two or three floors, constructed next to each other, having common walls, foundations and facilities. Also referred to as "terraced houses" in Singapore and Malaysia.

royalty A fee paid to the owner of land for extracting natural resources (oil, coal, etc.) from it.

ruko (*IDN*) Acronym for rumah-toko or shophouses.

rural Of or relating to the countryside, as opposed to cities.

saleable area The floor area exclusively allocated to the unit including balconies and verandahs but excluding common areas such as stairs, lift shafts, lobbies, etc. The saleable area is measured from the exterior of the enclosing walls of the units and to the center line of the party wall between two units.

salvage value The realizable value of goods or construction material that can be recovered and sold from a building that is being demolished. Example: doors, windows, marble slabs, steel rods, etc.

sangga imdaecha boho bup (*KOR*) Store Lease Protection Law. Given that the purpose of the Law is to protect the small business entities (whether individual or corporation) who lease their place of business, the maximum amount of security deposit to be defined in the Presidential Decree may not be high. The purpose of this law is to protect lessees of "store premises," and the basic features of the law are similar to those of the existing Residential Lease Protection Law, the purpose of which is to protect lessees of residential property and also commercial property as well.

sanheyuan (三合院) (*TWN*) It is a traditional Chinese residential property, so-called a "three-side enclosed courtyard," formed with inward-facing houses on three sides.

satellite cities Urban settlements that come up around a big city, that replicate on a smaller scale most of the amenities and facilities that are available in the big city. The main purpose of satellite cities is to decongest the main city around which they grow.

satisfaction The repayment in full of a debt or a payment in full and final settlement of an outstanding amount.

scale 1) Model depicting what a structure physically looks like. The dimensions are drawn on a proportionate basis to the real thing, such as 1:100 scale, which equals one centimeter to one meter. 2) A series of marks used in measuring or registering or comparing weights. 3) Peeling or flaking of a surface marked by discoloration.

science park A development of an industrial nature suited to accommodate high technology, with supporting amenities, which is often associated on site with or is close to a higher educational research establishment to provide cross-fertilization of ideas between entrepreneurs and researchers for the purpose of enabling academic knowledge to be applied to effective commercial use.

sea level The level of the surface of the sea; any surface on the same level with the sea.

seal(s) Identifier used on a document as a mark of genuineness and authenticity.

sealed bid An offer, usually in the form of a tender, submitted in a sealed package on the understanding that it will be opened simultaneously with other competitive offers at a stated time and place. In some circumstances tenderers are permitted to be present when the bids are opened.

search The reviewing, of all recorded transactions in the public record, to discover any title defects, which could interfere with the transfer of ownership of a property.

SEC (Securities and Exchange Commission) US federal agency created in 1934 to carry out the provisions of the Securities Exchange Act. Generally, the agency seeks to protect the investing public by preventing misrepresentation, fraud, manipulation and other abuses in the securities market.

second mortgage Mortgage that has second charge. This means that holders of a second mortgage will receive payment only after the first mortgage has been paid.

second-level market (二级市场) (*CHN*) The market where buyers purchase properties from the developers.

second-tier city (二级城市) Cities that are as large as many regional capitals in terms of size, but a step behind first-tier cities by way of comparing its property development cycle and sophistication of real estate market, as well as overall economic development. Wuhan, Nanjing, Hangzhou, Xian, Changsha, Suzhou, Chengdu and Dalian are generally considered to be second-tier cities.

secondary Property which is below that of prime in relation to rentals, location, etc.

secondary location Location that is less advantageous than desired.

secondary mortgage market The sale of a mortgagee's interest to third parties, usually banks and financial institutions. This provides liquidity to the mortgagee to make further advances to other parties. Such sales may fetch the mortgagee the full value of the loan it has advanced, but the usual practice is to sell such liens at a discount. A secondary mortgage market is distinct and different from a second mortgage and the two should not be confused. It can also refer to the sell down of interests in a property to multiple parties under various structures.

section A parcel of land whose boundaries are shown on a survey plan.

secured party A lender or a mortgagee whose interest is secured by a charge against a property.

securitization A financial technique whereby various types of obligations, typically mortgages but also car loans, credit card debt and others are, in effect, gathered into packages. This turns them into a tradable security, such as bonds, pass-through securities, REITs or collateralized mortgage obligations, which are sold to investors.

security agreement Any loan agreement that includes a charge on a fixed asset.

security deposit A deposit by a tenant kept with a landlord.

security interest The interest of a secured creditor.

seismic retrofitting (*JPN*) Retrofitting work done to existing structures to accommodate seismic requirements.

self-help If the landlord fails to perform his obligations as agreed and mentioned in the agreement within the stipulated time as mentioned in the agreement and such failure subjects persons or demised premises to an immediate risk of bodily harm or actual damage or causes a material and substantial delay in the business operations of the tenant, then the tenant will have the right to perform such obligation himself. The landlord will reimburse the tenant with the actual and reasonable costs of performing such obligation.

seller's market A market in any property or commodity where the circumstances are such that the seller has an advantage over a potential buyer to the extent that he can command a higher price than otherwise would be obtainable.

semi-detached house / bungalow (*SGP*) A type of landed housing whereby it comprises one half of a low rise detached building, usually not more than three storeys. The minimum plot size is 200 sq. m. and the minimum frontage is 8 m.

senior debt Debt that has priority for repayment in a liquidation.

SEPP (*AUS*) State Environmental Planning Policy is the overarching regional planning document at a regional, state level.

service charge The collective name for the cost of air-conditioning and other services and management charges passed on to the tenant.

serviced accommodation Fully furnished apartment where tenants are provided services such as housekeeping, security and concierge or reception or front office. Serviced apartments combine the features of a hotel and an apartment.

servient estate Land through which a right of way is given in favor of another land.

servitudes (地役權) (*TWN*) Servitude is the right to use the land of another person for the convenience of one's own land. The owner of the dominant land is entitled to perform such acts as are necessary for exercising or preserving his rights, provided that he shall choose the place and the method which will cause the least injury to the servient land. Furthermore, the owner of a dominant land, who makes constructions for the purpose of exercising his rights, is bound to maintain such constructions. The owner of the servient land may use the constructions as specified previously, except when it will obstruct the exercise of the servitude. In the case specified previously, the owner of the servient land shall bear his share of the expenses for the maintenance of the constructions in proportion to the interests he benefits therefrom.

settlement statement A complete and comprehensive statement on the total cost of a real estate deal.

shareholder The owner of shares in a company.

Shariah-compliant investment
*   **Ijarah** An Islamic lease agreement that allows the bank to earn profits by charging rentals on the asset leased to the customer.
*   **Murabahah** Purchase and resale. The capital provider purchases the desired commodity instead of lending money from a third party and resells it at a predetermined higher price to the capital user. By paying this higher price, the capital user has effectively obtained credit without paying interest.
*   **Sukuk** An asset-backed bond, similar to a conventional bond. A sukuk represents proportionate beneficial ownership in the underlying asset which will be leased to the client to yield the return on the investment.
*   **Musharakah** A partnership where profits are shared according to an agreed ratio while the losses are shared in proportion to the capital/investment of each partner.

    All partners of a business undertaking contribute funds and have the right, but not the obligation, to exercise executive powers in a musharakah. It is similar to a conventional partnership structure and the holding of voting stock in a limited company.

    This equity financing arrangement is regarded as the purest form of Islamic financing.
*   **Mudarabah** An investment partnership, whereby the investor (rab-ul-mal) provides capital to another party (mudarib) in order to undertake a business/investment activity. The profits are shared on a pre-agreed ratio, but the loss of investment is borne by the investor only.

The mudarib loses its share of the expected income. A mudarabah is similar to a diversified pool of assets held in a discretionary asset management portfolio.

- **Gharar** Uncertainty. This concept covers particular types of uncertainty or contingency in a contract. Gharar is often used as the grounds for criticism in Shariah Law of conventional financial practices such as short selling, speculation and derivatives.
- **Maysir** Gambling. This is often used as the grounds for criticism of conventional financial practices such as speculation, conventional insurance and derivatives.
- **Riba** Interest. This covers any financial return on money – whether the interest is fixed or floating, simple or compounded, and at whatever the rate.

shin-taishinkijun (*JPN*) New Aseismic Standard. Aseismic Standard is set based on several regulations including Building Standard Law and Notifications issued by the Ministry of Land, Infrastructure and Transport in 1981. Current Aseismic Standard is called as New Aseismic Standard, distinct as from the standard applied prior to 1981.

shintak (*KOR*) Trust.

shintaku juekiken (*JPN*) Beneficial interest in trust. The entitlement to receive benefits generated by assets held in another party's name, such as a trustee. In principle, beneficial interest in trust can be divided and transferred. Investors can take advantage of its lower transfer cost and credit insured characteristics in place of real estate transactions.

shohizei (*JPN*) Consumption tax. Consumption tax is imposed only on building and not on land. Consumption tax rate is 5%, applied to the transaction value for building.

shophouse (*SGP*) A low-rise building, usually less than four storeys, within a row of low-rise buildings whereby the ground floor is used for retail use and the upper floors are used for dwelling or commercial purposes.

shopping center/mall A large building, comprising several floors, housing several retail stores, food outlets, movie halls, etc., having a common parking area and under the same management.

short form document A document which refers to another document that contains all the details of an agreement.

side letter (*IND*) A document which refers to commercial term/s agreed between the parties, which cannot form part of the Leave & License Agreement/Lease Agreement as there would be implication of additional stamp duty or requirements by the licensors and his banks. Side letter is executed either on the landlords or tenants letter head or on a stamp paper.

signage Refers to anything that functions like a sign. The tenant and the landlord, on mutual discussion, will agree on the location for the tenant to erect their signage. Usually signage is provided by the landlord in the building directory and on the common lobby of the demised premises.

signed, sealed and delivered Legal phrase meaning that all requirements and formalities of a deal have been completed. The seal is normally used only by governments, corporate bodies, legal entities and notaries. Individuals only sign and deliver.

siheyuan (四合院) (*TWN*) It is a traditional Chinese residential property, or quadrangle, so-called a "four-side enclosed courtyard," formed with inward-facing houses on four sides, enclosed by walls. Such a residence offers space, comfort and privacy. A small or medium-sized siheyuan usually has its main or only entrance gate built at the southeastern corner of the quadrangle with a screen wall just inside to prevent outsiders from peeping in.

simple interest Interest that is paid on the principal amount alone.

Singapore Institute of Surveyors and Valuers (SISV) (*SGP*) SISV is the professional body representing the land surveyors, quantity surveyors, valuers, property managers, property consultants and real estate agents. Membership is divided into students, probationers, Member, Fellow and Honorary Fellow. To become a member, one must possess the relevant academic qualification that is recognized by the institute, appropriate practical experience and passing the Assessment of Professional Competence.

Singapore Land Authority (SLA) (*SGP*) The main focus of SLA is on land resource optimization, and it is responsible for the management of state land and buildings, land sales, leases, acquisitions and allocation, developing and marketing land-related information and maintaining the national land information database.

single family house A house that is designed for occupation by one family only, as opposed to an apartment block that is designed for occupation by several families.

single purpose property A building whose design precludes its use for any purpose other than the one for which it was originally built.

sinking fund A sum of money set aside at regular interval to earn interest on a compound basis either: 1) to be set off against the diminution in value of a wasting asset, e.g., a lease; or 2) to meet some future cash liability. In property valuations, it is usually assumed that the money will be invested at a "risk free" rate which is regarded as appropriate according to market conditions. The total amount calculated to accumulate by the sinking fund may be the same as the original investment or liability but possibly with an adjustment to reflect the view taken on future fluctuations in the value of money.

SIPPT (Surat Ijin Pendahuluan Penggunaan Tanah or location permit) (*IDN*) Required for development on a land with size equal or larger than 5,000 sq. m.

site analysis An examination of a property to decide if it is suitable for a particular use. Or an examination of a property with the purpose of deciding its most appropriate use.

site development Improvements made to a plot of land to make it suitable for building, such as leveling uneven ground, laying of sewer and underground utility lines, etc.

site plans Diagrams, sketches or maps showing the outline and location of a particular plot along with all features in it.

skin The exterior surface of a building.

sky lease A lease, securing exclusive use by a lessee and its nominees, of the air space above a plot of land. Example: nowadays, airport operators demand sky leases above the airports they develop or manage.

slab building (板楼) (*CHN*) Form of architecture, with only north and south orientation, which is good for taking in sunlight and has good ventilation, with usually no more than 12 floors.

small house (丁屋) (*HKG*) A three-storey house containing not more than 2,100 square feet built by eligible indigenous villagers in the New Territories.

Small Office Home Office (SOHO) 1) (*SGP*) SOHO are generally home offices where the occupants works and resides within the same place. SOHOs are also smart homes which provide occupants with the relevant communication and technological facilities to effectively run a business. 2) (*HKG*) The acronym for Small Office Home Office, this is a dual use development.

soft ratchet clause (*NZL*) A variation to the "ratchet clause," which allows for rental payable to reduce at a rent review but not below the rental payable at the commencement of the lease.

sole agency A sole agency precludes all other agents from working on the sale of the property, although another agent may approach the sole agent if it has a suitable party. The sole agent would handle the approach to the principal.

sole proprietorship Business that is owned by an individual. Unlike a private limited company which is a separate legal entity from an individual, the owner of a sole proprietorship is fully responsible for all the liabilities incurred by his business.

sole selling / letting rights The rights exercisable by an agent where the principal has contracted to convey wholly exclusive rights to sell/let the property, entitling the agent to commission even if the principal acts on his own behalf.

soyoo-kwon (*KOR*) Ownership.

space design Layout plan for the interior of a building. Involves both construction as well as interior designs.

span The distance between two pillars, walls or other load bearing structures.

square 1) Expressed in units of measuring area: square feet. 2) An open, usually four-sided area at the intersection of two or more streets, often planted with grass and trees for use as a park. 3) A rectangular space enclosed by streets and occupied by buildings; a block. 4) Something having an equal-sided rectangular form.

square foot The area contained by a square that is 1 foot long on all sides. The calculation is 1 foot x 1 foot = 1 square foot.

square foot cost The total cost of constructing a building divided by the total area in square feet.

square yard The area contained by a square that is 1 yard long on all sides. The calculation is 1 yard x 1 yard = 1 square yard, or, 3 feet x 3 feet = 9 square feet, 1 square yard = 0.8361 square meters.

stability certificate Issued by the government recognized consultant which states that the structural work of the building has been carried out in accordance with the structural consultants designs and drawings and the said structure is safe and stable for the purpose for which it is intended.

stamp duty A fixed tax chargeable on the execution of documents pertaining to certain transactions (e.g., leases).

stamp paper (*IND*) A legal paper on which stamp duty has been paid. The applicable amount of stamp duty paid on the documents in franked onto the legal paper, which shows the amount of stamp duty paid.

standard factory (*SGP*) A ready-built low rise (usually not more than two-storeys) factory building within an industrial estate that accommodates a wide range of light to medium industries that are non-pollutive and requiring heavy floor loading and large areas of ground floor space.

state land (*MYS*) All land in the state (including the bed of a river and of the foreshore and bed of the sea as within the territories of the state or the limits of the territorial waters) other than alienated land, reserved land and mining land.

state-level industrial park (国家级工业园区) (*CHN*) Development zones that carry the central government's guarantee that all incentives offered to investors have been pre-approved and certified by relevant government agencies.

state-owned housing (福利房) (*CHN*) Housing provided by the government for free, long ago as part of the welfare system, which could not be sold and transferred.

statute of limitations Law that stipulates that legal action to redress a wrongdoing has to be brought before a judicial forum within a set time, after which no legal remedy will be available.

statutory lien A lien or restriction created on the operation of land. Example: outstanding property taxes may create a lien against the property.

stock The total amount of space available within a given precinct. Buildings being refurbished and newly constructed space not yet available for occupation are excluded. The term generally includes buildings for owner-occupation in addition to those for leasing.

storm sewer Sewer that drains rainwater.

straight line depreciation Accounting terminology describing a system of depreciation where the value of the capital asset is written off (from the income generated by that property) by a uniform amount every year.

straight-term mortgage Mortgage where the principal amount is repaid only at maturity.

strata title Title to a horizontal part of a building with other freehold titles above and/or below. Satisfactory arrangements for management usually involve a statutory obligation for the setting up of a management corporation with responsibility for the maintenance of common facilities and areas.

strip center A shopping area, usually not enclosed and located off a major thoroughfare or highway with rows of retail outlets and common parking. It may or may not be under a single management.

sub-agent A person who receives and acts upon instructions from an agent, rather than from the principal.

sub-regional shopping center (*AUS*) An enclosed shopping mall anchored by two discount department stores and two supermarkets.

subcontractor A contractor engaged by a general contractor to execute specific jobs. The overall building contract is given to the general contractor, who then appoints electrical contractors, plumbing contractors, etc., to do specialized jobs.

subdivider A person who breaks up a large parcel of land into smaller plots with individual land titles and then sells them fully or in parts to others to build upon.

subdivision The division of a plot of land into smaller plots. Also means an administrative area smaller than a division.

subdivision map Detailed drawing of a real estate or administrative subdivision showing boundaries and other features.

subject to Conditional upon. For example, a buyer may agree to purchase a property subject to the existing title holder paying off all existing liens on it within a particular period.

sublease A lease granted by a person who himself enjoys only a lease interest over that property. Here, the sub-lessor cannot grant rights that he does not have. Example: A leases a plot of land to B for 25 years. If allowed in his contract with A, B can sub-lease the land to C for the remaining period of his lease term, but cannot sub-lease it for 26 years.

sub-lease space Vacant space which is available for lease from the contracted tenant of the premises.

subordinate To make something dependent on something else.

subpoena A summons issued by court.

suburban office market A commercial center offering decentralized office accommodation.

superficies (地上權) (*TWN*) Superficies is the right to use the land of another person with the object of owning a building or other works or bamboos or trees thereon.

supply New or refurbished space entering the market.

surrender The giving up of a right (such as a lease) with the agreement of both parties involved. Should not be confused with abandonment.

survey Measurement of the boundaries and topography of land.

survey number A portion of land of which the area and assessment are separately entered, under an indicative number in the land records maintained by the government.

sweat equity The appreciation in the value of property as a result of work done personally by the owner. Also means the issue of equity shares by an employer to an employee in recognition of good work done by the latter.

tacking 1) Adding a period of time onto another. For example: Adding periods of possession to add up to enough time for successful adverse possession. 2) Attaching a lien to a superior lien in order to gain the priority over an intermediate lien.

take out commitment Agreement by a lender to provide permanent financing following construction of a planned project.

take out loan The long term financing of a real estate after completion of the project.

takuchi tatemono torihikigyoho — takken gyoho (*JPN*) Real Estate Transaction Law. A law set for those who run real estate business to properly conduct its operation, to ensure fair real estate transaction, to promote a sound development of real estate business, to protect benefits of purchasers, and to facilitate the flow of real estate.

tax lien A lien placed on a property for nonpayment of taxes. Attaches only to the property upon which the taxes are unpaid.

tax shelter Tax advantages such as deductions for property taxes, maintenance, mortgage interest, insurance, and especially depreciation, which gives the owner certain tax advantages. An investment that offers income tax savings is called a tax shelter. A tax shelter acts as a form of tax incentive for any property that gives an investor the opportunity to claim losses or other deductions, or obtain benefits such as tax credits or revenue guarantees that over a stipulated period, are more than the amount the investor paid for the property.

technology park A landscaped development usually comprising high specification office space, laboratories, high technology engineering services and research and development facilities. It may include residential and retail developments, designed to encourage localization of high technology companies such as information technology, software development etc., thereby giving each the benefit of economies of scale. Usually, technology parks are located outside the inner city areas as these are quite land intensive in nature.

teiki shakuchi (*JPN*) Fixed-term Land Lease. The new Land and Housing Lease Act enacted in 1992 allowed a fixed-term land lease without extension under certain conditions. There are three types under the law and the most common lease law requires a set of conditions specifying the lease term of 50 years or more, prohibiting extension of lease term by reconstruction of the existing building and prohibiting the lessee to demand a buyback of the existing building.

teiki shakkaho (*JPN*) Fixed-term Lease Law (official name is Special Measures Law related to Promotion of High Quality Housing for Lease Supply). A special measures law enacted in 2000 to relieve the restrictions imposed on owners in order to expand the leasing market especially for residential properties. Japanese law had always protected the tenants by requiring owners to have a rightful reason to terminate the lease, but with this law, the term is fixed at the execution of agreement and it is not extended beyond the termination date.

temporary occupation license (*MYS*) A license issued by the state authority to occupy state land for certain restricted and permitted purposes for periods usually not exceeding one year (which can be renewed for a further year), unless for the purposes of extraction of rock materials for which terms of up to five years or more may be granted.

Temporary Occupation Permit (TOP) (*SGP*) The issue of TOP usually marks the building's physical completion as fit to stay. Only then can owners or tenants begin to occupy the premises. TOP is issued before CSC which denotes both legal completion and compliance with regulations.

tenancy 1) The right and the period of possession of real estate by ownership or rental. 2) (*MYS*) A rental agreement for a period not exceeding three years and not required to be registered on the title.

tenant Anyone, including a corporation, who rents real property, from the owner (called the landlord). The tenant may also be called the "lessee."

tenant for life A tenant who holds the lease for the entire tenure of his life.

tenant improvements Changes, typically to a property, to accommodate specific needs of a tenant. The cost of such improvements may be borne by the landlord or shared by both, the tenant and the landlord as may be agreed upon by the two.

tenant representative (TR) Agent who acts on behalf of a tenant, mainly in securing new rental accommodation and negotiating rental terms and reviews with the landlord.

tender 1) An offer of money or service in payment of an obligation. 2) A written offer to contract goods or services at a specified cost or rate; a bid.

tenure The length of time or condition under which something, such as a piece of property, is held. The duration of ownership rights.

term The period of time during which something is in effect. A stated number of years. A condition specified in an agreement.

term mortgage A mortgage where the interest is paid during the term and the total principal amount is to be paid in lump sum at maturity.

terminate Come to an end, conclude, cease, expire or lapse.

termination The legal right of the lessee/licensee to vacate the demised premises and terminate the agreement. The right to termination of lease/license is described in detail in the agreement.

terrace (*HKG*) A flat area of stone or grass outside a house.

terrace houses (*SGP*) A type of landed housing whereby several low rise houses, usually not more than three storeys, are linked together and they share common party walls. The minimum plot size is 150 sq. m. for the intermediate units and 200 sq. m. for the corner units. The minimum frontage of the buildings are 6 m. and 8 m. respectively.

Territorial Authority (TA) (*NZL*) City or District Council.

third party One who is not directly involved in a transaction or contract but may be involved or affected by it.

third-level market (三级市场) (*CHN*) Second-hand market for property.

third-tier city (三级城市) (*CHN*) Cities, in a broad sense, that are less economically developed and in which the real estate market is less sophisticated in terms of investment and development. These cities still have large quantities of raw land to be developed. The third-tier cities can include many cities at the provincial capital level. This category could include Guiyang, Hefei, Nanchang, Haikou, Urumchi, Hohhot, Lhasa, Dongguan, Zhongshan, etc.

time is of the essence Legal term which sets the time period within which a contract or certain Acts specified under a contract have to be executed.

time-sharing Ownership for a specific period of time, of a property, by several persons. Applicable to condominiums and resorts. For example a unit or apartment in a resort may be sold to 12 persons or entities where each is given the right to the unit for a period of one month every year. Weekly ownership is the most common period of time share.

title The legal right of an ownership interest in a property. Legal document which shows ownership of a piece of real estate.

title company Firm that provides insurance of a clear title once it completes its search for liens.

title insurance The policy that is issued to protect against loss due to a dispute in property ownership.

title search The reviewing, of all recorded transactions in the public record, to discover any title defects, which could interfere with the transfer of ownership of a property.

TMK (Tokutei Mokuteki Kaisha) (*JPN*) Japanese incorporated SPC (special purpose company) under the Law Concerning the Securitization of specified Assets (enacted in 1998) often used as the principal securitization vehicle.

tohkibo (*JPN*) Real Estate Registry Book. A public registry book stating required facts that clarify and preserve the existence of various legal rights and ownership in addition to recording the background. The first part of registry, "ko-ku" would have the legal right of ownership and "otsu-ku," the second part, would list legal rights other than the ownership pertaining to the subject real estate, such as a leasehold right or mortgage. In Japan, land and buildings are registered as separate real estate and a registry book is made for each.

toji (*KOR*) Land.

toji deunggi (*KOR*) Land title. An essential principle of the Real Property Registration Act is that the registration of an interest vests title in the registered proprietor of that interest. However, there is no guarantee of title by the government and any defect in one of the various instruments may affect title. All title information is contained in a Certificate of Title, issued and certified by the registry office. Dealings (transfer of ownership, mortgage, caveats or other interests) are recorded on the certificate and are secured and protected in the sequential order of registration.

tooja shintak company (*KOR*) Investment and trust company.

topographical survey A survey of an area by mapping the physical features of the region.

topography Art of mapping the physical features of a region. The topography describes the characteristics of an area, such as its contours, flatness, mountains, etc.

Torrens Title (*AUS*) A title registration system. Named after Sir Robert Torrens, a British administrator of Australia, this system allows the condition of the title to be discovered without resorting to a title search.

tort Damage, injury, or a wrongful act done willfully, negligently, or in circumstances involving strict liability, but not involving breach of contract, for which a civil suit can be brought.

toshi keikakuho (*JPN*) Urban Planning Law. A law enacted to promote sound and orderly development of a city. It comprises nine zones including Urbanization Promotion Area and Urbanization Restriction Area.

toshikeikakuzei (*JPN*) City Planning Tax. City Planning Tax is levied on land and buildings located in certain urban areas as a surcharge to the Fixed Asset Tax. The annual standard tax rate is 0.3%, applied to the asset value for Fixed Asset Tax purpose.

total occupancy cost A tenant's total expenditure on its premises.

tower building (塔楼) (*CHN*) One form of architecture, which has elevators in the central core of the building, and apartments located around it in all directions, in which the floor plate is like a square. This design is suitable for multi-storey construction.

townhouse A dwelling unit, generally having two or more floors plus a garage and is attached to other similar units via party walls. Such dwellings are typically found in condominiums and cooperatives or as part of a planned unit development.

townhouse (*SGP*) A residential building designed as a single dwelling house unit with ground contact and forming part of a row of not less than three residential units with common ownership of land.

tract A parcel of land generally held for subdividing and development into residential units.

trade fixtures Articles of personal property installed in rented buildings by the tenant to help carry out a trade or business. Trade fixtures are removable by the tenant before the lease expires and are not true fixtures.

traffic count The number of pedestrians or vehicles moving past a given point in a given period of time. The traffic count of pedestrians entering a shopping mall is an indication of its popularity and patronage. The higher the figure, the higher the potential for shopper spending in the shopping mall.

traffic density Usually expressed as vehicles per kilometer or mile of road, a survey of traffic moving across a portion of road at a given point of time.

transaction costs Taxes, legal fees and other costs incurred in transacting property.

transfer tax An assessment and imposition of tax by state or local government when a piece of property changes hands.

transparency (market) Degree of clarity regarding the operation of financial, legal, tax and other systems in a market.

triple a grade The highest specification of building available in the market.

triple net A lease where the lessee has to pay all expenses of the property leased including maintenance, in addition to a fixed rent.

trust A legal arrangement by which a person or entity (the trustee) has legal control over certain property (the trust property or trust corpus), but is bound by fiduciary duty to exercise that legal control for the benefit of someone else (the beneficiary), according to the terms of the trust and the law. Thus, in a trust the legal ownership that the trustee has is split from the equitable or beneficial title that the beneficiary has. The trustee holds only the bare legal title to the property.

trust account Special account that is used to safeguard the funds of a buyer or seller.

trust deed Legal term which sets the time period within which a contract or certain Acts specified under a contract have to be executed.

trustee 1) One, such as a bank, that holds legal title to property in order to administer it for a beneficiary. 2) A member of a board elected or appointed to direct the funds and policy of an institution. 3) A country responsible for supervising a trust territory.

trustee in bankruptcy Person selected by a judge or creditors of a bankrupt individual to handle matters including the sale of the bankrupt's assets, management of the funds from the sale of those assets, payment of expenses, and distribution of the balance to creditors. The trustee is usually compensated with a specified percentage of the liquidation sale.

trustee's sale A foreclosure sale conduced by a trustee under the stipulations of a deed of trust.

Truth in Lending Act (*PHL*) A law that requires lenders to report or disclose the cost of credit in terms of annual percentage rate.

tsubo (*JPN*) Tsubo is a unit for area in Japan most commonly used in reference to real estate; one tsubo equals 3.305785 square meters.

turn key A development in which a developer completes the entire project on behalf of a buyer. All the new tenant or owner has to do is "turn the key" to the apartment or office in a newly constructed building because everything is completed and ready for occupancy.

turnover 1) The number of times a particular stock of goods is sold and restocked during a given period of time. 2) The amount of business transacted during a given period of time. 3) The number of workers hired by an establishment to replace those who have left in a given period of time. 4) Gross revenue or total sales of a business entity.

turnover rent A rent that is calculated as a percentage of the turnover of the lessee's business. Often used in leases of shop space for major chain stores in a shopping mall. Usually, the turnover rent is applied in addition to a base rent or is structured to take effect when the lessee's turnover reaches a certain figure mutually agreed between the landlord and the lessee.

UCV (*AUS*) Unimproved capital value, or sometimes referred to as land value (LV) is the basis upon which property taxes are assessed by local authorities. It represents the value of the underlying land before capital improvements are undertaken.

under construction Refers to a development where actual building construction has been initiated.

under floor wiring system Wires, for example electrical, which are placed beneath the flooring of a structure through conduits or raceways.

under improvement An improvement which because of its deficiency in size or cost is not the highest and best use of the site.

under-lease A lease granted by a tenant or lessee; especially, a lease granted by one who is himself a lessee for years, for any fewer or less number of years than he himself holds; a sublease.

underpass An underground tunnel or passage enabling pedestrians to cross a road or railway.

underpinning Reinforcement of a building with supports or the use of beams temporarily while the structure is being built.

underwriter One who signs a policy of insurance, by which he becomes an insurer. By this act he places himself as to his responsibility, in the place of the insured. He may cause a re-insurance to be made for his benefit; and it is his duty to act with good faith, and, without quibbling, to pay all just demands against him for losses.

undivided shares (*HKG*) An important element of the system of co-ownership devised for multi-storey buildings in Hong Kong. Each owner of the individual units in a multi-storey building has an equal undivided share as tenant in common with all other co-owners of the government land lease. The owner has an exclusive right of possession of his unit but he shares the common parts of the land with all other owners.

uniform system of accounts for hotels A standardized system of accounting, with set formats and account classifications, used in the hospitality industry. It allows easy comparison of the financial and operational performances of two or more hotels. The original standard was set by the New York chapter of the International Association of Hospitality Accountants (IAHA) in 1926. IAHA is now called Hospitality Financial & Technology Professionals.

unimproved land Raw land in its natural state that has no installed improvements or structures.

unit Segregated part of a structure, i.e., one apartment in an apartment building or an office in a commercial building.

unit cost The cost of a single item on a construction budget. The unit cost is multiplied by the number of units required for the job to determine the total cost. May also refer to the cost expressed on a per unit basis e.g. $ x per square foot.

unit title Individual ownership for multi owner properties such as high rise office blocks, apartment buildings and industrial units.

unity of interest Joint tenants have to acquire their interest by the same conveyance and the said interest must remain the same.

unity of possession Equal rights to possession of the entire property by joint tenants.

unrealized gain/loss The difference between the cost (or previously reported fair market value) of an asset held at the balance sheet date and its fair market value at that date.

unrenovated property (毛坯房) (*CHN*) Apartments that do not have finishings or fittings. This is the norm for most apartments built by local mainland Chinese developers in secondary cities whereas developments by foreign developers tend to provide finished or semi-finished apartments, some with bathroom and kitchen fittings and appliances.

urban Relating to a city or a town.

Urban Redevelopment Authority (URA) (*SGP*) The Urban Redevelopment Authority (URA) is Singapore's national land use planning authority. URA prepares long term strategic plans, as well as detailed local area plans, for physical development, and then co-ordinates and guides efforts to bring these plans to reality.

urban renewal Old and obsolete property of a city or town that has been improved or modernized or demolished and replaced.

use density The ratio of the number of buildings or floor area of built-up space of a particular use to a given area.

use value The value of a property in terms of a specific use.

useful life 1) Life of property used for depreciation accounting, which does not necessarily coincide with the actual physical life. 2) The actual economic worth of a property in terms of years of use to the owner.

user An individual who uses a property or has a right over a property.

usury Levy of excessive rate of interest on a loan that is considered illegal as it is not accepted by law.

utilities Services such as water, gas, electricity, etc., provided to land or houses by public or private utility companies.

utility charges Utilities such as water and power for the demised premises is separately charged/metered to the tenant. The tenant is usually responsible to pay to the concerned utility company the charge for such utilities as per the bills raised by the utility company.

utility room Room that contains the appliances necessary for the maintenance of that establishment such as a room used for laundry, heating equipment telephone wiring, janitorial purposes, etc.

vacancy A house or apartment or shop space or office space that is available for rent or sale.

vacancy factor The ratio of vacant space, expressed as a percentage, in a building or project.

vacancy rate Ratio of vacant space to total stock in the market.

vacant land Land without structures.

vacant possession Vacant possession is delivered when the buyer is allowed to use the property immediately without anyone else still living in it or using it.

vacate To move out of a house, apartment, office, retail or industrial space.

valuable consideration Legal term meaning money has been paid as part of a contract. The term valuable does not imply any particular value.

valuation 1) The process of making an estimate of the worth of real property or other assets for a particular purpose, e.g., letting, purchase, sale, audit, rating, compulsory purchase or taxation. That purpose and the relevant circumstances will determine assumptions and facts that are appropriate and hence the process used. 2) A statement, usually in writing, setting out the facts, assumptions, calculations and resultant value. 3) Colloquially, the value arrived at as a result of the valuation process.

value The financial worth of a thing.

value for sale under repossession The price that might reasonably be expected to realize within 90 days from the sale of the property in the market under repossession by the lender or receiver, on an "as is" basis, taking into account the unique quality of the property and the existence of any specific demand as well as factors which might adversely affect the marketability of the property due to market perception of increased risk or stigma, justified or otherwise. The term replaced "forced sale value" and "estimated restricted realization price."

value-added tax (VAT) Value-added tax is a form of sales tax. It is a tax on consumption levied on the sale of goods and services and in the Philippines, on the import of goods. It is an indirect tax, which can be passed on to the buyer.

variable air volume (VAV) The air-conditioning system provided in the majority of modern buildings. A set temperature with tenant controlled volume.

variation A change to a service or product from the original specification.

vendee Opposite of vendor, buyer.

vendor Seller.

veneer Thin covering that is fixed to the item being covered.

village Small rural (usually farming) community that lives in a cluster of huts or houses in close proximity to each other.

VP (*AUS*) Vacant possession, describes the sale of a property not encumbered by any occupational leases.

volatility In regard to real estate, refers to the size of the fluctuation in prices or returns.

WACC/WALE (*AUS*) Used by investors and financiers to assess property risk and cost/return considerations. The terms reflect weighted average cost of capital being the blended returns of debt and equity, and weighted average lease expiry being the analysis of lease terms by area and by income.

waive To give up, renounce, submit or surrender a right, benefit, privilege or claim.

waiver Refers to a legal document that proves the relinquishment of rights or claims. It may also mean deliberate relinquishment of rights or claims.

walsei (structure) (*KOR*) Monthly rental structure that requires an initial security deposit equivalent to 10 months' rent, in addition to a monthly rent and maintenance charge. It is a very common rental structure.

WALT (*NZL*) Weighted average lease term – the unexpired lease term in a property or portfolio weighted by the net lettable area or income applicable to each lease.

warehouse Building that is used specifically for the purpose of storing or keeping merchandise.

warehousing The act of holding mortgages for the purpose of later securitizing and selling the same to other investors or lenders.

warrant Legal assurance that the conveyed title is good and the possession of the same will be undisturbed.

warranted price contract An agreement between parties to design and construct a facility for a maximum price to an agreed brief where any savings may be shared between the parties.

warranty Legally binding agreement given at the time of a sale, by the seller to the buyer, containing certain assurances as to the terms and condition of the property being sold.

water rights The legal right of a landowner to the water found on his property.

water table Level of water saturation in the ground. The depth at which natural underground waters are found.

waterfront Property with a body of water in front of it. Alternately, a contiguous area of similar properties near a large body of water which has a commercial port.

watershed Land area where water collects. The term may be used to describe a dividing point that sends water runoff flowing into different drainage areas.

wayleave An easement or right to cross land.

wear and tear Deterioration or decline in the value of a property due to use, physical damage, old age or environmental factors.

weathering The wear and tear of the exterior of a building caused by exposure to weather.

wing Building part, which is connected to, but leading away from the main structure.

withholding tax A tax payable to the state on the sale, transfer or other disposition of real estate classified as ordinary asset.

without prejudice A phrase used to enable parties to negotiate an agreement or settle a dispute, either orally or in writing, without any statement or admission made being subsequently quoted or produced in evidence at any legal hearing bearing on the subject-matter of the proposed agreement or dispute. In claiming this privilege, care must be taken to avoid statements which are untrue or of a defamatory nature, which might entitle the court to allow their admission in evidence at the request of the other party. In any event, the privilege applies only to the proceedings in question, so that "without prejudice" statements (verbal or written) can, in certain circumstances, be produced in evidence in some other, unrelated, dispute.

without recourse A company is not responsible to a third party when an account or financial instrument is not honored by the debtor with the creditor's only recourse being to the debtor's property.

working capital Assets available for use in the production of further assets. May include cash or liquid assets.

working drawing A drawing made to scale with details and markings to facilitate use by builders and engineers during construction.

workspace ratio Average space allocated to each worker in an organization.

writ of ejectment Court order allowing a landlord to evict a tenant because of non-payment of rent or damaging property. The writ contains needed instructions and directs an officer of the court to execute it.

writ of execution Court order allowing the seizure and sale of property due to non-payment of taxes or foreclosure of property.

Written Permission (WP) (*SGP*) The approval granted by the minister for National Development or the competent authority to develop any land subject to conditions in accordance with the development rules in force.

written-down value The book value of an asset after accounting for depreciation and amortization.

wuzheng（五证）(*CHN*) A summary term for five key certificates, including land use right certificate, land use planning approval, building plan approval, construction permits and pre-sale certificate.

yangdo (*KOR*) Assignment.

yard 1) A measure of length, equaling three feet, 36 inches or 0.9144 meters. 2) An enclosure; usually, a small enclosed place in front of, or around, a house or barn; as, a courtyard; a front or back yard; a barnyard. 3) An enclosure within which any work or business is carried on; as, a dockyard; a shipyard.

yield The return on an investment compared to the total cost of investment over a given period of time; e.g., if an investment of $1,000 gives returns of $100 in one year, the yield on the investment is 10%.

YK (yugen kaisha) (*JPN*) Japanese form of a limited liability company under business law.

yosekiritsu (*JPN*) Floor area ratio.

yotochiiki (*JPN*) Zoning. Zoning regulations restrict the building types, purpose, size in each district. There are 12 districts: Type I & II low-rise residential; Type I & II mid-high-rise residential; Type I & II residential; quasi residential; neighborhood commercial; commercial; quasi industrial; industrial; and industrial exclusive districts.

Z

zone Geographic location with designated boundaries such as a district. May also refer to a specific land use within a designated boundary or area as part of the master plan for a large scale development such as a township. E.g., residential zone, industrial zone or commercial zone, etc.

Appendix 1

Metric Conversion Chart

US Units	Multiplied By	Equals Metric Units		Metric Units	Multiplied By	Equals US Units
Length						
Inches	2.54	Centimeters		Centimeters	0.3937	Inches
Feet	0.3048	Meters		Meters	3.2808	Feet
Yards	0.9144	Meters		Meters	1.0936	Yards
Miles	1.6093	Kilometers		Kilometers	0.6214	Miles
Area						
Square inches	6.4516	Square centimeters		Square centimeters	0.155	Square inches
Square feet	0.0929	Square meters		Square meters	10.764	Square feet
Square yards	0.8361	Square meters		Square meters	1.196	Square yards
Acres	0.4047	Hectares		Hectares	2.471	Acres
Volume						
Cubic feet	0.0283	Cubic meters		Cubic meters	35.3144	Cubic feet
Cubic yards	0.7646	Cubic meters		Cubic meters	1.3079	Cubic yards
Gallons	3.7854	Liters		Liters	0.2642	Gallons
Weight						
Foot-pounds	1.383	Newton-meters		Newton-meters	0.738	Foot-pounds
Pounds	0.4536	Kilograms		Kilograms	2.2046	Pounds
Foot-pounds	1.383	Newton-meters		Newton-meters	0.738	Foot-pounds

Asian Units	Multiplied By	Equals Metric Units
Mu (亩)	666.67	Square meters
Tsubo	3.305785	Square meters
Pyong	3.3088	Square meters
Chia (甲)	0.96992	Hectare
Ping (坪)	3.305	Square meters

Appendix 2

Asia Pacific Market Practice – Property Taxes

Country	VAT/GST Payable on Rent & Service Charge	Other Property Tax for Tenants
Australia	10% GST	Local government rates and land tax are charged to the building owner and recovered from tenants through the outgoings charge.
China	None	Other property tax is usually borne by the landlord.
Hong Kong	None	Government rates are indirect taxes set by the government. Rates are usually paid by the landlord and charged back to the tenant on a quarterly basis. Rates are currently at 5% of rateable value to the property.
India	None	Other property and municipal taxes are usually included in rent or service charge.
Indonesia	10% VAT on rent 10% VAT on service charge 2% to 6% withholding tax	Other property tax is usually borne by the landlord.
Japan	5% consumption tax	Fixed assets tax and city planning tax are paid to the municipality by the registered owner of lands and/or buildings as at January 1 of each year. They are included in the rent and are not charged separately to the tenant.
Malaysia	None	Assessment and quit rent are a form of property tax levied on the landlord who recovers it via the service charge for the tenant as a proportional basis.
New Zealand	12.5% GST	Municipal (Local Government) Rates is a property tax set by the local government. It can either be charged to the tenant or to the landlord for recovery from the tenant.
Philippines	10% VAT	Other property tax is usually borne by the landlord.
Singapore	5% GST	Tenants occupying property on leases of less than 7 years are usually not liable for property tax. However, it is common practice for landlords to insert a clause within leases which requires tenants to pay to the landlord any increase in property tax that is required statutorily.
South Korea	10% VAT	Property tax is payable by owners of buildings as at the base date of assessment and is usually charged back to the tenant in the form of rent or service charge.
Taiwan	5% VAT	House tax and land value tax are borne by the landlord.
Thailand	7% on service charge & furniture rental	Other property tax is usually borne by the landlord.
Vietnam	10% on rent and service charge	Other property tax is usually borne by the landlord.

Appendix 3

Country	Lease Term	Rental Payments						Service charges, Repairs & Insurance		
	Typical Lease Length	Frequency of rent payable (In Advance)	Rent Deposit (expressed as x months rent)	Statutory Right to Renewal and Service Charge	Basis of Rent Increases or Rent Review	Frequency of Rent Increases or Rent Review	Internal	Common Parts (reception, lifts, stairs etc)	External/ structural
Australia	3-5 years	Monthly	1 month	No	Open market rental value/ Fixed	Annually	Tenant	Landlord charged back via service charge	Landlord charged back via service charge
China	2-3 years	Monthly	2-3 months	No	Open market rental value	At lease renewal	Tenant	Typically landlord charged back via service charge	Typically charged back via service charge
Hong Kong	3-6 years	Monthly	2-3 months (gross rent)	No	Open market rental value	At renewal or 3 yearly in longer leases	Tenant	Typically landlord charged back via service charge	Typically landlord charged back via service charge
India	2 years (plus option to extend for 3-5 years)	Monthly	8-12 months	No	Fixed increase 15% - 20% every 3 years or 7% per annum. Occasionally negotiable.	3 yearly	Tenant	Landlord charged back via service charge*	Landlord charged back via service charge*
Indonesia	3 years (up to 6 or 10 years for larger tenants)	Quarterly	3 months (gross rent)	No	Open market rental value (upward only and negotiable)	3 yearly or at renewal	Tenant	Typically landlord charged back via service charge	Landlord unless proof that tenant caused damage
Japan	2 years	Monthly	12 months	(auto renewal)	Open market rental value	At lease renewal	Tenant	Landlord	Landlord
Malaysia	3 years (plus option to extend for 3 years)	Monthly	2-3 months (gross rent)	No	Open market rental value	3 yearly	Tenant	Landlord charged back via service charge	Landlord charged back via service charge
Myanmar	1-year - locally owned building 1-3 years - foreign owned building	Annually (some landlords may accept 6 months)**	3 months (gross rent)	No (yes- for foreign owned buildings)	Open market rental value (with a cap of 25% increase)	3 yearly	Tenant	Landlord charged back via service charge	Landlord charged back via service charge

Taxation			Disposal of Leases		
Building Insurance	Local Property Taxes	VAT Payable on Rent	Assignment/ Sub-letting	Early Termination	Tenant's Building Reinstatement Responsibilities At Lease End
Landlord charged back via service charge	Landlord charged back via service charge	GST - 10%	Typically yes	Only by break clause	Original condition allowing for wear and tear
Typically landlord	Landlord	None	Generally accepted (subject to landlord approval)	Only by break clause	Original condition allowing for wear and tear
Landlord charged back via service charge	Landlord charged back via service charge	None	Sub letting occasionally to 15-20% assignment-prohibited	Only by break clause (not common)	Original condition
Landlord charged back via service charge*	Landlord	None	Allowed for subsidiaries and affiliates	Negotiable with lock-in period (3-6 months notice)	Original condition allowing for wear and tear
Landlord charged back via service charge	Landlord charged back via service charge	10% on rent +10% on service charge	Typically yes (subject to landlord approval)	Only by break clause (negotiable, subject to penalty)	Original condition allowing for wear and tear
Landlord charged back via service charge	Landlord	5%	Typically prohibited	At 6 months notice	Original condition
Landlord charged back via service charge	Landlord (In some cases if there is any increase, Landlord will pass the cost to the tenant via an increase in service charge)	None	Generally accepted (subject to landlord's approval)	Only break clause (not common)	Original condition allowing for wear and tear
Landlord charged back via service charge	None	None	Generally accepted (subject to landlord approval)	Yes (subject to penalty clause)	Original condition allowing for wear and tear

Appendix 3 – *cont'd*

Country	Lease Term	Rental Payments					Service charges, Repairs & Insurance		
	Typical Lease Length	Frequency of rent payable (In Advance)	Rent Deposit (expressed as x months rent)	Statutory Right to Renewal and Service Charge	Basis of Rent Increases or Rent Review	Frequency of Rent Increases or Rent Review	Internal	Common Parts (reception, lifts, stairs etc)	External/ structural
New Zealand	6-9 years	Monthly	2 months (gross rent)	No	Open market rental value (with ratchet)	3 yearly	Tenant	Landlord charged back via service charge	Landlord charge back service charge (except for structural repairs)
Philippines	3-5 years	Quarterly/ Monthly	3 months (gross rent)	No	Fixed % increase or market rental value	Annually or at renewal	Tenant	Landlord charged back via service charge	Landlord charged back via service charge
Singapore	3 years	Monthly/ Quarterly	3 months (gross rent)	No	Open market rental value	At lease renewal	Tenant	Landlord charged back via service charge	Landlord charged back via service charge
South Korea	2-3 years with 1 year extensions implied	Monthly*	10 months or Chonsei	Depends on lease	Open market rental value at LL's discretion, some indexing also	Annual	Tenant	Landlord charged back via service charge	Landlord
Taiwan	3-5 years	Monthly/ Quarterly	3-6 months	Depends on lease	Open market rent or subject to negotiated arrangement	Annual	Tenant	Landlord charged back via service charge	Landlord sometimes charged back via service charge
Thailand	3 years	Monthly	3 months	No	Open market rental value	At lease renewal	Tenant	Landlord	Landlord
Vietnam	3 years	Monthly/ Quarterly	3-6 months (gross rent)	No	Open market rental value	At lease renewal	Tenant	Landlord charged back via service charge	Tenant

Notes:

India
* Generally service charge is inclusive of all costs. A breakdown of costs is not applicable apart from the most modern buildings.

Myanmar
* There are no standard practices currently in place in Myanmar. The first building of an international standard has been completed in January 1998 and the above information has been based on this. **This is for a locally developed building for a forreign

South Korea
* 'Chonse' leases have no monthly rent. Rent is derived from the landlord's use of the deposit and term of the lease.

* Rental payments are typically paid on gross area (adjusted for efficiency) except for Australia and Singapore (which are on surveyed area).

Taxation			Disposal of Leases		
Building Insurance	**Local Property Taxes**	**VAT Payable on Rent**	**Assignment/ Sub-letting**	**Early Termination**	**Tenant's Building Reinstatement Responsibilities At Lease End**
Landlord charged back via service charge	Landlord charged back via service charge	12.50%	Generally accepted (subject to restrictions)	Only by break clause (not common)	Original condition allowing for wear and tear
Landlord charged back via service charge	Landlord	10%	Generally accepted (subject to landlord approval)	Only by break clause with penalties	Original condition allowing for wear and tear
Landlord charged back via service charge	Landlord	5%	Sub-letting Normally yes assignment- occasionally permitted	Only by break clause (not common)	Original condition allowing for wear and tear
Landlord	Landlord	10% but refundable annually	Usually prohibited (subject to landlord approval)	Negotiable (depends on lease)	Original condition allowing for wear and tear
Landlord	Landlord	5%	Prohibited (but occasionally to affiliates)	Yes (subject to penalty clause)	Original condition allowing for wear and tear
Landlord charged back via service charge	Landlord	7%	Usually prohibited	Only by break clause	Original condition allowing for wear and tear
Landlord charged back via service charge	Landlord	None	Prohibited	Only by break clause	Original condition allowing for wear and tear

Appendix 4

Country	Grade A
Australia	High quality space with good views/outlook, quality lobby finish, quality access, attractive street setting, quality presentation and maintenance. Building intelligence; direct building controls, 24-hour access with card key and off cite alarm monitoring, key switch after hours air-conditioning.
China - Beijing	As per Hong Kong, but total building size larger than 25,000 sq. m., & located in major business area district.
China - Shanghai	High quality finishes; Quality construction; Large floor plate (1,000 sq. m. above); Flexible layout; Spacious lobbies and circulation areas; Effective central air conditioning (HVAC); Professional building management; Access to major roads and metro system; Adequate car parking facilities; Average or above efficiency ratio (60-65%; Basic back up power system; Adequate lift provisions; Adequate washroom facilities; Adequate information infrastructure to support phone and data systems.
Hong Kong (1)	Modern with high quality finishes; flexible layout; large floor plates; spacious, well decorated lobbies and circulation areas; effective central air-conditioning; good lift services zoned for passengers and goods deliveries; professional management; parking facilities normally available.
India	Flexible and large floor plates; spacious, well-decorated lobbies and circulation areas; effective central air-conditioning; well-managed building or professionally management; parking facilities normally available; good tenant profile.
Indonesia	Flexible and large floor plates; spacious, high quality modern finishes of building's interior and exterior; high standard installed Building Automation Systems (BAS); sufficient back-up power; well-managed building or professionally management; adequate parking facilities; good accessibility; good tenant profile.
Japan (2)	Total leasable floor area: 10,000 sq. m. + Typical leasable floor area per floor: 800 sq. m. + Building height: 60 m. + Completion: later than 1982 with some exceptions Ceiling height: - 2650 mm. + Lobbies/public space: Well appointed & spacious.
Philippines	High quality building located within the CBD, building age, professionally managed, 100% back-up power, building specification, good tenant mix/profile.
Singapore (3)	As per Hong Kong.

(1) Hong Kong Rating & Valuation Department Definition. Please note that location is not a feature of grade.
(2) JLL Research - Tokyo Definitions
(3) No government definitions

Country	Grade A
Taiwan	Quality of Finish: Top quality finish immediately obvious when entering the building/floor. The presence of natural light is also important. Age: There is no exact age limit for grade A property, but older buildings should be examined more closely before classifying them as grade A stock. Location: While location is important, and most grade A buildings will be in CBD areas, location alone neither qualifies, nor disqualifies a building for grade A status. Ceiling Height: 2.4M minimum. Floor Plate Minimum: As with total size, there is no exact size requirement, but generally the floor plate should be approximately 300 pings (10,600 sq. ft.). Floor Loading: 500 kg per square meter. Earthquake Code Compliance: Grade A buildings should comply with current earthquake compliance code. Currently compliance is not strictly enforced, and only owners who apply for an assessment will be able to certify compliance. This issue is likely to become important in the near future. Parking: Grade A buildings should have adequate parking facilities relative to its size. Infrastructure: Building must be facing a road witth a 30 m. width or greater and have good access to a highway or MRT line. Ownership: The building need not be owned by a single owner/group (strata title is acceptable), but the owners need to be able to make consensus agreements that do not interfere with building management. Management: Professional, competent building management dedicated to keeping the facilities and appearance of the building top rate. Tenant Roster: The tenant roster should reflect a facility that is well regarded and respected. Considerable latitude is given here, but decreases in tenant roster could indicate changing perception of the building's quality. Services (Fiber optic backbone/Lifts/Elevators/Central Air/Power Supply/Fire Safety). Infrastructure for telecommunications must be available; Sufficient for tenant use; Air temperature and quality control is essential; Adequate and dependable; Building must have smoke detectors and sprinkler systems and be in compliance with fire codes.
Thailand	Floor plate: a) regular shape, b) without structural encumbrances, c) can be easily subdivided, d) large size (greater than 1,000 sq. m.). Air-conditioning: a) central chiller, typically with VAV system, b) separate 24-hour air-conditioning for tenant computer rooms. Building Management: a) Professional building management, b) good safety and security system, c) Building Automation System (BAS). Car Parking: a) Minimum 1 space/100 sq.m., b) effficient entry and exit, c) security system/guards in parking area. Common Areas: High quality internal and external finishes. External typically steel frame, glass heat-reflective curtain wall. Internal typically polished granite or marble common areas. Lifts: Efficient lift system, (standard min. peak waiting < 30 secs) zoned for high-rise buildings b) separate service lift. Telecom: Fibre optic, ISDN; trunking floor system. Ceiling Height: Min. 2.7 m. Common areas: Restrooms & AHU rooms in common area. Fire & Safety: a) 2 fire exits/floor, b) air-pressurized staircase. Amenities: Retail facilities, eateries and other conveniences located in building and surrounding area. Age: Typically less than 15 years old.

Appendix 4 – *cont'd*

Country	Grade B
Australia	Good quality space with a reasonable standard of finish and maintenance. Building intelligence; with electronic controls, 24-hour access with key cards and switch for after hours air-conditioning.
China - Beijing	Same as Hong Kong, location in accessible area with easy public transport.
China - Shanghai	Older buildings; Ordinary design with dated finishes; Smaller floor plates; Average building systems; Average lift services; Average property management; Below average efficiency ratio; Limited parking facilities.
Hong Kong (1)	Ordinary design with good quality finishes; flexible layout; average-sized floor plates; adequate lobbies; central or free-standing air-conditioning; adequate lift services, good management; parking facilities not essential.
India	Flexible and average sized floor plates; adequate lobbies; no central air-conditioning; adequate lift services; average management; average tenant profile.
Indonesia	Smaller floor plates; average building systems; older buildings; ordinary design; average building systems; mostly in-house property management; limited parking facilities; limited back-up power.
Japan (2)	Typical leasable floor area per floor: 660 sq. m. Completion: later than 1982 with some exceptions. Ceiling height: less than 2600 mm. Lobbies/public space more limited with basic finishes.
Philippines	Good quality building located within or near the CBD, building age, not professionally managed, 50% back-up power, average handover condition, average tenant mix.
Singapore (3)	As per Hong Kong.
Taiwan	Please see the definition in the "Grade A" column. If the building cannot meet at least 80% of the qualifications, they will be considered as B grade buildings.
Thailand	Floor plate: a) regular shape, b) minimal structural encumbrances, c) flexible layout, d) Average size (900-1,000 sq. m. Air-conditioning: a) central chiller, b) constant air volume from a water cooled system, c) separate 24 hour air-conditioning for tenant computer rooms. Building Management: Good building management. Managed by international property management companies or equivalent services by building owners or other service providers. Car Parking: a) Minimum 1 space/100 sq. m., b) efficient entry and exit. Common Areas: Main entrance and floor lobbies with ordinary design and mid-quality finishings. Lifts: a) allocated to different zones, b) separate service lift, c) slightly longer wait time than Grade A. Ceiling Height: 2.6 m. Amenities: Some retail facilities, eateries and other conveniences located in building and/or in immediate area. Age: Typically 10-20 years old.

(1) Hong Kong Rating & Valuation Department Definition. Please note that location is not a feature of grade.
(2) JLL Research - Tokyo Definitions
(3) No government definitions

Country	Grade C
Australia	Older style office space with lower quality finish. Building intelligence; electronic building controls.
China - Beijing	As per Hong Kong definition.
China - Shanghai	N/A
Hong Kong (1)	Plain with basic finishes; less flexible layout; small floor plates; basic lobbies; generally without central air-conditioning; barely adequate or inadequate lift services; minimal to average management; no parking facilities.
India	Plain with basic finishes; less flexible layout; small floor plates; basic lobbies; no central air-conditioning; barely adequate or inadequate lift services; minimal to average management; barely adequate or inadequate parking. Average tenant profile.
Indonesia	Small floor plate; mostly with no central AC systems; minimal management; low to average quality of building's exterior and interior, no BAS; limited parking; very minimum of back-up power.
Japan (2)	No definition – Typically floor plates less than 660 sq. m.
Philippines	Low building quality and specification, basic handover condition, no back-up power.
Singapore (3)	As per Hong Kong.
Taiwan	Not Available.
Thailand	Floor plate: a) irregular shape, b) structural encumbrances, c) difficult to subdivide d) small size (less than 900 s.m.) Air-conditioning: a) inefficient air-conditioning system b) no central air-conditioning or split-type (air cooled package). Building Management: a) Poor building management, b) in-house, c) poor safety and security system, d) Building Automation System (BAS). Car Parking: a) Less than 1 space/100 sq. m. b) insufficient parking available, c) entrance & entry to parking is difficult. Common Areas: a) Small lobby area, b) plain finishes, b) floor lobbies plain. Lifts: a) not allocated to different zones/zoned in larger groups, b) no separate service lift, c) long wait times. Ceiling Height: below 2.5 m. Common Area: Restroom & AHU are in the leased space. Fire & Safety: No sprinklers in the leased space. Flooring: Vinyl tile. Amenities: minimal amenities in building or area. Age: Typically greater than 20 years old.

(1) Hong Kong Rating & Valuation Department Definition. Please note that location is not a feature of grade.
(2) JLL Research - Tokyo Definitions
(3) No government definitions

Glossary of Asia Pacific countries

AUS – Australia

API Australian Property Institute (professional body).

Building Code of Australia (BCA) sets minimal building standards.

confidentiality agreement (CA) This is a common document used by vendors prior to releasing confidential information to prospective purchasers. It often carries the full weight of the law if breached.

curtilege The area of land around improvements required for the effective operation of those improvements eg., access ways, driveways, gardens etc.

floor space ratio (FSR) Similar to the definition of plot ratio, it describes the relationship between land area and permissable gross floor space allowable under the local planning code.

Listed Property Trust (LPT) This term describes the securitized listed property sector in Australia, commonly referred to as REITs in other countries. It is one of the largest most sophisticated securitized property markets in the world and dominates the Australian investment landscape. They are essentially tax efficient vehicles where small and large investors can own a slice of an income producing real estate portfolio by buying and selling units (or shares) on the stock market. LPTs are traditionally passive low-risk structures but are increasingly offering investors higher returns through exposure to riskier activities such as development, land banking, accessing debt and other financial balance sheet engineering.

loan to value ratio (LVR) Reflects the relationship between value and borrowings. Financial institutions use this to assess lending risk.

Local Environmental Plans (LEP) Local Environmental Plans form the basis of all local authority planning schemes in Australia.

mortgagee in possession The position a lender takes in repossessing a property where the lender is in default of its loan obligations.

Moving Annual Turnover (MAT) This is a term used to analyze the performance of retail shopping centers and more specifically the running turnover (or consumer spend) levels reported by retailers in major shopping centers.

negative gearing It is a financial tool utilized by Australian investors whereby the cost of borrowing less the income received can be offset against taxable income from other investment sources. This makes property an attractive investment asset class.

PCA Property Council of Australia (peak industry lobby group).

put option A legal document requiring the purchaser to acquire an interest in property if activated by the vendor.

regional shopping centre An enclosed shopping mall anchored by at least two department stores, two discount department stores and two supermarkets.

SEPP State Environmental Planning Policy is the overarching regional planning document at a regional, state level.

sub-regional shopping centre An enclosed shopping mall anchored by two discount department stores and two supermarkets.

Torrens Title A title registration system. Named after Sir Robert Torrens, a British administrator of Australia, this system allows the condition of the title to be discovered without resorting to a title search.

UCV Unimproved Capital Value, or sometimes referred to as Land Value (LV) is the basis upon which property taxes are assessed by local authorities. It represents the value of the underlying land before capital improvements are undertaken.

VP Vacant Possession, describes the sale of a property not encumbered by any occupational leases.

WACC/WALE Used by investors and financiers to assess property risk and cost/return considerations. The terms reflect weighted average cost of capital being the blended returns of debt and equity, and weighted average lease expiry being the analysis of lease terms by area and by income.

CHN – China

business tax（营业税） Business tax is levied at 5% on gross rental income for property leases and 5% on total sales value for property sales.

city maintenance and construction tax（城市维护建设税） It is levied at 1-7% of business tax, depending on location and local government.

courtyard（四合院） English term used for "siheyuan." The siheyuan is a traditional architectural style in Chinese culture. A siheyuan consists of a square housing compound, with rooms enclosing a central courtyard. In China, traditional courtyard housing is often one-storey.

first-tier city（一级城市） Cities that are first market entry-points for most foreign companies. Its office markets have quality facilities, professional property management, and its markets have a degree of sophistication in property purchasing and leasing. These are generally said to be Beijing, Guangzhou, Shanghai and Shenzhen.

hutong（胡同）Traditional Chinese neighborhood, in which pingfang or courtyards are connected by walls.

land appreciation tax（土地增值税）It was introduced in January 1994 and implemented in 1995.

land classification（土地分类）According the location of the land, the government divided the land into ten different categories, in which there is a different price for each. Land zoned for residential, commercial, industrial use will fall into one of these categories.

mature land（熟地）Land that has been developed for use and has utilities already installed, such as gas connections, electrical hook-up, water and sewage lines, etc.

mu（亩）An area measurement unit in China, 15 mu = 1 hectare, 1 mu = 666.67 sq. m.

overseas Chinese（海外华人）People of Chinese ethnicity whose primary nationality is not Chinese. That is, they are residents and citizens of other countries. Overseas Chinese have been known to be significant economic driving forces for several countries in South East Asia. With the opening up of China to foreign investments, overseas Chinese from Hong Kong, Taiwan, Singapore and Thailand are known to bring their investments, skills and spending power into China, fuelling its economic development.

pingfang（平房）Chinese bungalow, which is an older type of housing accommodation in China, with one-storey and usually of poor quality.

renovated property（装修房）Apartments in China that are fully finished and fitted out with wardrobes, bathroom fittings, cabinets and floor finishes. Typically targeted at middle and high-income families in major cities such as Beijing, Shanghai, Guangzhou, Shenzhen but are also being introduced into fast-growing cities such as Suzhou and Hangzhou by foreign developers as they raise the standard of residential developments in these cities.

second-level market（二级市场）The market where buyers purchase properties from the developers.

second-tier city（二级城市）Cities that are as large as many regional capitals in terms of size, but a step behind first-tier cities by way of comparing its property development cycle and sophistication of real estate market, as well as overall economic development. Wuhan, Nanjing, Hangzhou, Xian, Changsha, Suzhou, Chengdu and Dalian are generally considered to be second-tier cities.

slab building（板楼）Form of architecture, with only north and south orientation, which is good for taking in sunlight and has good ventilation, with usually no more than twelve floors.

state-level industrial park (国家级工业园区) Development zones that carry the Central Government's guarantee that all incentives offered to investors have been pre-approved and certified by relevant government agencies.

state-owned housing (福利房) Housing provided by the government for free, long ago as part of the welfare system, which could not be sold and transferred.

third-level market (三级市场) Second-hand market for property.

third-tier city (三级城市) Cities, in a broad sense, that are less economically developed and in which the real estate market is less sophisticated in terms of investment and development. These cities still have large quantities of raw land to be developed. The third-tier cities can include many cities at the provincial capital level. This category could include Guiyang, Hefei, Nanchang, Haikou, Urumchi, Hohhot, Lhasa, Dongguan, Zhongshan, etc.

tower building (塔楼) One form of architecture, which has elevators in the central core of the building, and apartments located around it in all directions, in which the floor plate is like a square. This design is suitable for multi-storey construction.

unrenovated property (毛坯房) Apartments that do not have finishings or fittings. This is the norm for most apartments built by local mainland Chinese developers in secondary cities whereas developments by foreign developers tend to provide finished or semi-finished apartments, some with bathroom and kitchen fittings and appliances.

wuzheng (五证) A summary term for five key certificates, including land use right certificate, land use planning approval, building plan approval, construction permits and pre-sale certificate.

HKG – Hong Kong

accommodation value (AV) A unit rate of site value or land price, obtained by dividing the site value or land price by the floor area of the proposed development on the site.

adverse possession Possessory title to land which is gained by occupying the land for a specific period of time, without the interference of the land owner.

application list List of government lands announced by the government, out of which developers may apply for the sale of the sites via public auction.

certificate of compliance (滿意纸) A certificate issued to the registered owner of property when the Director of Lands is satisfied that all the positive obligations imposed by the general and special conditions in the land lease governing the lot have been complied with.

cockloft An upper loft, a garret or the highest room in a building.

contractor's method Valuation by aggregating the estimated land value and the estimated construction costs of a replacement building. This method is used for specialized or non-profit making properties where there is no market.

deed of mutual covenant (公契) **(DMC)** A contract entered into by the developer of the land, the building manager and the first party to purchase a unit in the development. The DMC sets out the details for the management and regulation of the multi-storey building and the details of the distribution of and equal and undivided shares in the land.

Demarcation District During the period 1898 to 1904, a survey was carried out in the New Territories using relatively simple methods. This survey resulted in the production of about 600 map sheets known as Demarcation District (DD) sheets. These sheets show individual lot boundaries but without any grid reference to facilitate locating them on the ground. The plans were prepared at a scale of 16 inches or 32 inches to the mile (i.e., 1/3960 or 1/1980 respectively). Boundaries are shown graphically without any dimension and the accuracy of these sheets was relatively low. Lot areas were scaled off the DD sheets and the smallest unit of 0.01 acre was adopted for recording purposes.

government rates (差餉) Rates are a tax on the occupation of property, and are charged at a percentage of the rateable value of property. The current percentage is 5% (2006).

government rent (地租) The rent payable by the land owner to the government under the land lease. The government rent could be a lump sum rent or 3% of the rateable value of the property, depending on the type of the land lease.

gross development value The aggregate capital value of the stratified units of the proposed development assuming completion of construction as at the date of assessment.

industrial/office building A dual-purpose building in which every unit of the building can be used flexibly for both industrial and office purposes. In terms of building construction, the building must comply with all relevant building and fire regulations applicable to both industrial and office buildings, including floor loading, compartmentation, lighting, ventilation, provision of means of escape and sanitary fitments.

industrial estate In the three industrial estates in Hong Kong, The Hong Kong Science and Technology Park offers developed land at cost to both manufacturing and service industries with new or improved technology and processes which cannot operate in multi-storey factory or commercial buildings.

occupation permit（入伙紙）A permit issued by the Building Authority to certify that a building (the construction of which is governed by the Building Ordinance) can be occupied.

Outline Zoning Plan（分區計劃大綱圖）Statutory plans prepared under the Town Planning Ordinance which depicts the land use zoning.

small house（丁屋）A three-storey house containing not more than 2,100 square feet built by eligible indigenous villagers in the New Territories.

SOHO concept The acronym for Small Office Home Office, this is a dual use development.

terrace A flat area of stone or grass outside a house.

undivided shares An important element of the system of co-ownership devised for multi-storey buildings in Hong Kong. Each owner of the individual units in a multi-storey building has an equal undivided share as tenant in common with all other co-owners of the government land lease. The owner has an exclusive right of possession of his unit but he shares the common parts of the land with all other owners.

IND – India

hard option Option on a certain area of premises (i.e., 100 sq. ft. or 1,000 sq. ft. or 100,000 sq. ft.) offered by the lessor to the lessee over a fixed duration of time where in the lessor will not market the area to another tenant/party for that specific time frame. A hard option can either be free of cost or could have a holding cost of a bear minimum value.

holding cost A fixed amount paid to the lessor for predefined time frame (i.e., Hard Options Period).

incubation space Fully fitted out interim space offered by the lessor/developers to the lessee/tenant for a short duration of three to 12 months till the permanent space/building is ready and operational. Sometimes available in Science Parks and Business Parks to assist or encourage Research & Development start-ups or to nurture small businesses.

Leave & License An agreement recording a license between a licensor and licensee. The term of the license should not exceed 60 months. This kind of agreement is specific to Bombay (Mumbai) where corporates would enter into a Leave & License Agreement instead of a Lease Agreement to save on the Stamp duty and registration charges. A Leave & License agreement is usually for a period of 36 months.

NRI Non-Resident Indian. This refers to an Indian who is a citizen and resident of other countries. Non-Resident Indians often return to India on periodic visits because of family or business ties and are known to bring investments, skills and spending power which helps to foster India's economic development.

registered agreement A Leave & License Agreement/Lease Agreement which has been adequately stamped with the applicable stamp duty and then registered with the sub-registrar.

registration Every Leave & License Agreement/Lease Agreement in India has to be registered with the office of the sub-registrar of assurances (local authority) for it to be enforceable by law. This is the obligation of the licensor/lessor/landlord. However, the cost towards registration of the agreement is usually paid by the licensee/lessee.

ROFR Right of first refusal (ROFR) is provided by the lessor to the lessee on an additional area which has not been committed by the lessee. The lessor on finding another interested tenant for the area will provide the lessee with an opportunity to take up the area within a specified number of days, if the lessee does not take up the area within the specified number of days, the lessor will go ahead with the interested tenant.

side letter A document which refers a commercial term/s agreed between the parties, which cannot form part of the Leave & License Agreement/Lease Agreement as there would be implication of additional stamp duty or requirements by the licensors and his banks. Side letter is executed either on the landlords or tenants letter head or on a stamp paper.

stamp paper A legal paper on which stamp duty has been paid. The applicable amount of stamp duty paid on the documents in franked onto the legal paper, which shows the amount of stamp duty paid.

IDN – Indonesia

AJB (Akte Jual Beli) Deed of release (of land title).

BKPM Investment Coordinating Board.

BPHTB Transfer tax which is payable for any real estate transaction.

BPN (Badan Pertanahan Nasional) National Land Agency.

Dinas Tata Kota Town Planning Authority.

Hak Guna Bangunan (HGB) Most common land title (proof of ownership for 20 to 30 years and extendable).

Hak Guna Usaha Right of Exploitation.

Hak Milik Equivalent to freehold interest.

Hak Pakai Right of Use.

Hak Pengelolaan Right to Operate.

Hak Pengelolaan Lahan Right to manage land, generally granted to government entities.

Ijin Mendirikan Bangunan (IMB) Building permit (all buildings should have this permit).

inbreng Contribution in kind.

kawasan industri Industrial estate.

KDB Site coverage ratio.

kios Units in strata titled shopping center.

KLB Floor area ratio.

KPR (Kredit Pemilikan Rumah) Home mortgage financing.

mal Shopping center.

materai Stamp duty.

nilai buku Book value.

PBB (Pajak Bumi Bangunan) Real estate tax.

Pejabat Pembuat Akte Tanah (PPAT) Generally notaries who are authorized to produce land deeds.

Pengikatan Perjantian Jual Beli (PPJB) Sale and purchase binding agreement for a real estate transaction.

penilaian Appraisal.

perkantoran Office building.

perumahan Residential estate.

PTUN Administrative court.

ruko Acronym of rumah-toko or shophouses.

SIPPT (Surat Ijin Pendahuluan Penggunaan Tanah or location permit) Required for development on a land with size equal or larger than 5,000 sq. m.

JPN – Japan

hoshokin / shikikin Security deposit. A monetary deposit paid to the lessor by the lessee, usually several months' rent amount CAM charge not included, to be returned at the termination of lease. As a form of guarantee, it can be used to offset any debt by the lessee, such as payment delinquency.

kenchiku kinjunho Building Standard Law. A law that sets the minimum building standards associated with structural safety, building coverage, floor area ratio, height and fire codes for the purpose of protecting the lives, well-being and assets of the citizen and to promote social welfare.

kenpeiritsu Building to land ratio.

kenrikin / reikin Key money. Key money in "reikin" form varies by the region, however its origin was a token of gratitude paid to the lessor by the lessee for signing the lease. In the Kanto area, it is usually two months rent, but in Kansai there is no key money. Key money is not returned. Key money in "kenrikin" form usually applies to commercial properties, sometimes to land parcels, originally paid as a "good will" fee for operating the business in the building. It is also fundamentally non-returnable.

KK (kabushiki kaisha) Japanese public corporation under business law.

kohshin Contract renewal. In essence, this is an extension of the existing lease. Without a termination notice within a period specified in the agreement, the contract is automatically renewed. Some fixed-term agreements are exceptions. Upon contract renewal for a residential property, the lessee pays a certain amount to the lessor as a "renewal fee."

koji-chika Refers to the prices of land at selected sample spots in the country issued by the Ministry of Land, Infrastructure and Transport every March. It is used as an indicator for transaction as well as benchmark for valuation.

koteishisanzei Fixed Asset Tax. Fixed Asset Tax is levied on land, buildings and depreciable assets used for business purposes as of January 1st every year. Fixed Asset Tax is levied by the municipality where the fixed assets are located. The annual standard tax is 1.4%.

ku (ward) Precinct unit applied in larger cities.

kubunshoyu tatemono Strata Title or Partial Ownership of a Building. The ownership granted on portions that are deemed independent within a building used for residence, retail, office, warehouse, etc., whether vertical or horizontally divided.

kyoekihi CAM charges. Fees charged on top of monthly rent of a building and its site. Generally includes water, utilities, cleaning, repair, maintenance, security and air-conditioning fees.

PML (probable maximum loss) An index used to assess the risk of possible damage a structure may incur in the event of natural disaster, more specifically earthquake. It is included in the engineering report in the due diligence procedure and the lower the number, the more earthquake-tolerant the structure.

rosenka Refers to the prices of land at selected sample spots on major streets in the country issued by the National Tax Agency. It is used to assess inheritance and gift taxes and is normally assumed at 80% of the value (*Koji-chika*) issued by the Ministry of Land, Infrastructure and Transport.

seismic retrofitting Retrofitting work done to existing structures to accommodate seismic requirements.

shin-taishinkijun New Aseismic Standard. Aseismic Standard is set based on several regulations including Building Standard Law and Notifications issued by the Ministry of Land, Infrastructure and Transport in 1981. Current Aseismic Standard is called as New Aseismic Standard, in distinction from the standard applied prior to 1981.

shintaku juekiken Beneficial interest in trust. The entitlement to receive benefits generated by assets held in another party's name, such as a trustee. In principle, beneficial interest in trust can be divided an transferred. Investors can take advantage of its lower transfer cost and credit insured characteristics in place of real estate transactions.

shohizei Consumption tax. Consumption tax is imposed only on building and not on land. Consumption tax rate is 5%, applied to the transaction value for building.

takuchi tatemono torihikigyoho — takken gyoho Real Estate Transaction Law. A law set for those who run real estate business to properly conduct its operation, to ensure fair real estate transaction, to promote a sound development of real estate business, to protect benefits of purchasers, and to facilitate the flow of real estate.

teiki shakuchi Fixed-term Land Lease. The new Land and Housing Lease Act enacted in 1992 allowed a fixed-term land lease without extension under certain conditions. There are three types under the law and the most common lease law requires a set of conditions specifying the lease term of 50 years or more, prohibiting extension of lease term by reconstruction of the existing building and prohibiting the lessee to demand a buyback of the existing building.

teiki shakkaho Fixed-term Lease Law (official name is Special Measures Law related to Promotion of High Quality Housing for Lease Supply). A special measures law enacted in 2000 to relieve the restrictions imposed on owners in order to expand the leasing market especially for residential properties. Japanese law had always protected the tenants by requiring owners to have a rightful reason to terminate the lease, but with this law, the term is fixed at the execution of agreement and it is not extended beyond the termination date.

TMK (Tokutei Mokuteki Kaisha) Japanese incorporated SPC (special purpose company) under the Law Concerning the Securitization of specified Assets (enacted in 1998) often used as the principal securitization vehicle.

tohkibo Real Estate Registry Book. A public registry book stating required facts that clarify and preserve the existence of various legal rights and ownership in addition to recording the background. The first part of registry, "Ko-ku" would have the legal right of ownership and "Otsu-ku," the second part, would list legal rights other than the ownership pertaining to the subject real estate, such as leasehold right or mortgage. In Japan, land and building are registered as separate real estate and registry book is made for each.

toshi keikakuho Urban Planning Law. A law enacted to promote sound and orderly development of a city. It comprises nine zones including Urbanization Promotion Area and Urbanization Restriction Area.

toshikeikakuzei City Planning Tax. City Planning Tax is levied on land and buildings located in certain urban areas as a surcharge to the Fixed Asset Tax. The annual standard tax rate is 0.3%, applied to the asset value for Fixed Asset Tax purpose.

tsubo Tsubo is a unit for area in Japan most commonly used in reference to real estate; one tsubo equals 3.305785 square meters.

YK (yugen kaisha) Japanese form of a limited liability company under Business Law.

yosekiritsu Floor area ratio.

yotochiiki Zoning. Zoning regulations restrict the building types, purpose, size in each district. There are 12 districts: Type I & II low-rise residential; Type I & II mid-high-rise residential; Type I & II residential; quasi residential; neighborhood commercial; commercial; quasi industrial; industrial; and Industrial exclusive districts.

KOR – Korea

bojeungbu walsei (hybrid structure) A rental system that incorporates a blend of the chonsei and walsei rental structure. Includes a higher than normal security deposit (less than chonsei however) and a lower monthly rent than a walsei rent. Service charge is still due on a monthly basis.

bojeunggum (lease key money) Security deposit. Under the lease, a bojeunggum is payable upon signing the lease and normally equivalent to 10 times the monthly rental amount in the case of walsei rental structure. This amount shall be deposited without any interest rate during the lease term and can be increased during rental reviews throughout the term of the lease, but the total amount is returned to the tenant at the expiration of the lease.

boodongsan Real estate.

booga gachi-se (value-added tax) VAT at the rate of 10% is applied to the supply of goods and services by a taxable entity. "Goods" includes the supply of buildings and "services" includes the supply of the contractual or legal right to use the goods.

boonyang Sales for strata title.

chaebol A large business conglomerate.

chae-kwon Bond.

chonsei (structure) Traditional Korean rental method that involves depositing a large upfront amount (approximately 60-70% of the purchase value) and leasing the space without paying any monthly rent, service charges are due monthly.

chonsei-kwon A chonsei right is very similar to a kun-mortgage. Like the mortgage, the chonsei right comes into effect upon registration. However, unlike a mortgage, in the event that title to the premises is transferred to a third party, the chonsei right holder can continue to occupy and use the premises for the remainder of the existing term, except as against a party taking title in connection with foreclosure proceedings involving mortgagee claims that have priority over the chonsei right holder. In the event that the landlord fails to refund the key money deposit, the chonsei right holder may enjoy many of the rights enjoyed by a mortgagee, i.e., the right to foreclose upon the premises, etc. The time and procedures required for the foreclosure proceedings are also similar to that required for foreclosing against a mortgage. One significant difference is that the registration of a chonsei right may only be made with respect to a key money lease arrangement. Another difference is that a chonsei registration must be renewed every time the lease term is renewed.

daeriin Attorney in law.

deunggi Official registration by the government.

dosi gyehok-se City planning tax. Persons who own land or houses within area announced by the mayor or country commissioner as an area for the assessment of city planning tax are liable to pay tax on the value of the land or house at a rate of 0.2% or 0.3%.

ga-deunggi Provisional registration.

gamjung Real estate valuation (or appraisal).

gongdong shisul-se Community facility tax. Persons benefiting from the provision of fire service facilities, garbage disposal, sewerage, or similar facilities are subject to a tax of 0.06% - 0.16%.

gubun deunggi Strata-title (partial ownership of the building). Based on the concept of the horizontal and vertical sub-division of airspace enabling land and buildings to be sub-divided into lots with a separate individual title to each lot. The ownership and management of multi-unit buildings are regulated, through which the creation of an agent management body is required. As "agent" for the proprietors of the multi-building unit lots, the body is responsible for the maintenance and management of the building.

gunmul deunggi Building title.

gunpye-rul (rate) The building-to-land ratio.

gwanribee Service charges (maintenance fees). This includes air conditioning, electricity for common areas, security, gas, taxes, insurance and other services (varies throughout market)· Payable in addition to chonsei and walsei amounts.

gyouk-se Education tax. This is payable by the taxpayer of Property Tax and Aggregated Land Tax pursuant to the Local Tax Law at a rate of 20% of the Property Tax and Aggregated Land Tax.

imdae cha Lease.

jaesan-se Property tax. Payable by owners of buildings as at the base date of assessment. The tax base is the current "Standard Value" of the building as determined by the relevant local government and the tax rate varies, depending on the type of property.

jeondae Sub-lease.

jeonhwan-rul (rate) Conversion rate chonsei to walsei. Chonsei amount can be converted to monthly rental by applying a conversion rate. These rates ranging from 12% to 18% are applied to obtain the conversion rate.

jeonyong-rul (rate) Building efficiency rate (net to gross ratio). Critical to Korea as rental is charged based on the gross area. The tenant is responsible for paying a portion of common areas that include lift lobbies, corridors, bathrooms and stairwells.

jihap gunmul Multi-unit building.

jonghap toji-se Aggregated land tax. This is payable on all types of land by the owner of such land as of the base date of assessment. The tax base is the "standard value" and the general rate, which covers the most common categories of land, varies progressively from zero.

kun-judang-kwon A kun-mortgage. This is a special type of mortgage unique to Korea. It may be used to secure any type of debt. It is distinctive in that it secures the debt at its maximum amount without regard to intermediate increases or decreases in the amount of the debt. If the amount of principal outstanding plus interest at any given time falls below the secured amount, the full amount of the debt, but no more, will be secured by the mortgage. But if the amount of principal outstanding plus interest at any given time exceeds the stated maximum amount, then such excess will not be secured. Accordingly, it is advisable to fix the maximum amount at a level that exceeds the principal of the claim amount. Customarily such maximum ranges from 110-130% of the principal amount. Since a kun-mortgage is indivisible, the mortgagee may exercise its right over the whole property covered by the mortgage until its claim has been completely satisfied. Mortgagees are paid according to priority, which is generally determined at time of registration.

kunmul Building.

kwonrigum Premium.

pyung It is a traditional standard measurement unit of area used in Korea. Its use is limited to real estate. 1 pyung = 3.3058 sq. meter = 35.58 sq. ft.

sangga imdaecha boho bup Store Lease Protection Law. Given that the purpose of the Law is to protect the small business entities (whether individual or corporation) who lease their place of business, the maximum amount of security deposit to be defined in the Presidential Decree may not be high. The purpose of this law is to protect lessees of "store premises," and the basic features of the law are similar to those of the existing Residential Lease Protection Law, the purpose of which is to protect lessees of residential property and also commercial property as well.

shintak Trust.

soyoo-kwon Ownership.

toji Land.

toji deunggi Land title. An essential principle of the Real Property Registration Act is that the registration of an interest vests title in the registered proprietor of that interest. However, there is no guarantee of title by the government and any defect in one of the various instruments may affect title. All title information is contained in a Certificate of Title, issued and certified by the registry office. Dealings (transfer of ownership, mortgage, caveats or other interests) are recorded on the certificate and are secured and protected in the sequential order of registration.

tooja shintak company Investment and trust company.

walsei (structure) Monthly rental structure that requires an initial security deposit equivalent to 10 months' rent, in addition to a monthly rent and maintenance charge. It is a very common rental structure.

yangdo Assignment.

MYS – Malaysia

accessory parcel Means any parcel shown in a strata plan, which is used in conjunction with a parcel.

alienate land To dispose of state land in perpetuity or for a term of years, in consideration of the payment of rent, otherwise in accordance with the provisions of Sections 76 of the National Land Code 1965.

assessment A form of building tax, which is payable to the local authority. This tax is calculated as a percentage of annual value and varies with the property type.

boundary mark Any survey stone, iron pipe, or spike, wooden peg or post, concrete post or pillar or other mark used for the purpose of making boundaries.

express condition A condition created and explicitly stated within a land title stipulating the condition of the use of a land.

Malay Reserve Land Land reserved for alienation to Malays or to natives of the State in which the land lies.

proprietor Any person or body for the time being registered as the proprietor of any alienated land.

quit rent Land tax levied on property owners, which varies from one state to another, payable to the land office. The rate for quit rent also varies with land category and size.

reserved land Land reserved for a public purpose for the time being.

restriction in interest Means a limitation imposed by the state authority on any of the powers conferred on a proprietor of land, normally on the use of the land.

state land All land in the state (including the bed of a river and of the foreshore and bed of the sea as within the territories of the state or the limits of the territorial waters) other than alienated land, reserved land and mining land.

temporary occupation license A license issued by the state authority to occupy state land for certain restricted and permitted purposes for periods usually not exceeding one year (which can be renewed for a further year), unless for the purposes of extraction of rock materials for which terms of up to five years or more may be granted.

tenancy A rental agreement for a period not exceeding three years and not required to be registered in the title.

NZL – New Zealand

building warrant of fitness An annual certificate signed by the building owner or manager saying that requirements under the compliance schedule for the property have been met.

certificate of title A document attesting to the rights of ownership to a piece of land describing the land involved, the area, the legal description, the type of ownership and any listed mortgages, charges, leases, easements and other encumbrances.

code of compliance certificate Certificate issued when building work is completed confirming that the construction complies with the New Zealand Building Code.

compliance schedule A local council document listing the inspection, maintenance and reporting procedures for safety systems such as fire alarms and lifts to ensure they are safe to use.

cross lease When each owner has an equal undivided share of the land but leases their own site and building from all the land owners.

deposited plan A survey plan giving legal definition to property boundaries.

district plan A document, generally consisting of maps, policies and rules which sets out the activities permitted on any land governed by a district or city council.

Land Information Memorandum (LIM) A report issued by a city or borough council, listing all the information that the council has about the property including what building consents and code of compliance certificates have been issued.

NZIV New Zealand Institute of Valuers.

NZPI New Zealand Property Institute.

PCNZ Property Council of New Zealand.

PCNZ guide for measurement of rentable areas A formula for the measurement of rentable areas, devised by PCNZ (Property Council of New Zealand) and generally accepted as the methodology to be applied in the country.

phoenix company A company that goes into voluntary liquidation to avoid litigation then re-emerges essentially as the same company, but under a different name.

Project Information Memorandum (PIM) A report issued by the local council prior to issuing a building consent, confirming that building work may proceed, subject to any of the requirements under legislation.

REINZ Real Estate Institute of New Zealand.

resource consent A land use consent, issued under the Resource Management Act, by a local council.

soft ratchet clause A variation to the "Ratchet Clause," which allows for rental payable to reduce at a rent review but not below the rental payable at the commencement of the lease.

Territorial Authority (TA) City or District Council.

WALT Weighted average lease term – the unexpired lease term in a property or portfolio weighted by the net lettable area or income applicable to each lease.

PHL – The Philippines

escheat Reversion of private property to the state due to the intestate death of the owner who does not have any legal heir; or confiscation of illegally acquired property.

Truth in Lending Act A law that requires lenders to report or disclose the cost of credit in terms of annual percentage rate.

SGP – Singapore

annual value (AV) AV is used as the basis to compute property tax for most types of properties in Singapore. AV is the gross rental value which a property is expected to fetch when let and less what the landlord pays for expenses of repair and maintenance.

Building Construction Authority (BCA) The primary role of BCA is to develop and regulate Singapore's building and construction industry. BCA issues the TOPs and CSCs, approve structural plans and permit building works.

Building Plan approval (BP) This refers to the approval granted by the Commissioner of Building Control in respect of building plans and specifications submitted in accordance with the prescribed building regulations in force. BP approval is needed before construction can begin and before a sales license can be granted.

caveat A legal notice lodged with the Registrar of Titles to prevent the registration of land title until the claim of the lodger has been determined.

Central Provident Fund (CPF) The CPF is a comprehensive social security savings plan which has provided many working Singaporeans with a sense of security and confidence in their old age. CPF is contributed by both the employee and employer and can be used for purchase of properties, investments as well as healthcare, although the actual withdrawal of CPF can only be done at age 55.

Central Provident Fund Board A statutory board in charge of the administration of CPF. It also sets the percentage of distribution to the various accounts as well as the percentage contribution from employees and employers.

Certificate of Statutory Completion (CSC) A certificate issued by the building authority to certify that all building works have been completed in accordance with regulations.

cluster housing Cluster housing is a hybrid development which combines conventional housing with the features of condominium housing with strata titles, shared facilities such as swimming pools, landscaped gardens and other amenities but within a low-rise building form usually not exceeding 4 storeys in height.

collective (en-bloc) sales An arrangement whereby owners of separate units of a private residential project or even commercial building pool their interests together and sell them collectively to a developer.

common property Any premises not included in the strata lot but within the strata-titled development. Examples of common property would include communal facilities like swimming pool and clubhouses as well as areas like lift lobbies and staircases.

compulsory acquisition Governed by the Land Acquisition Act, the State may acquire land for public interest or benefit.

Concept Plan The Concept Plan is the long-term plan for Singapore's physical development for the next 40-50 years. The Concept Plan lays the foundation for the drafting of the Master Plan and was completed with extensive inputs from the public. It is revised every 10 years.

Confirmed List (Government Land Sales Program) Under the Government Land Sales program, sites which appear on the Confirmed List would be put up for sale by tender as scheduled.

conservation houses Conserved buildings are selected by Urban Redevelopment Authority based on their historical and architectural significance, rarity in terms of building types, styles, and their contribution to the overall environment. There are also certain guidelines which restricts the use and additions and alterations (A&A) works that can be done on the conserved building.

Deferred Payment Scheme (DPS) This is a flexible payment scheme subject to limits imposed by the Controller of Housing. It requires the purchaser to exercise his option by signing the Sale & Purchase Agreement within three weeks of booking a unit and paying 5% of the purchase price as the booking fee. The remaining 5% (or 15%, depending on the loan quantum) of the downpayment is payable by the purchaser within 8 weeks from the date of the Option. The rest of the purchase price may be deferred upon obtaining TOP or any time before that.

detached houses/bungalow A type of landed housing where by it comprises a detached dwelling house, usually not more than three storeys. The minimum plot size is 400sqm and the frontage is 10m.

development charge/differential premium A levy imposed when planning permission is granted to carry out development on a site for a more intensive use; change of use or higher plot ratio. Development charges are applicable to freehold land while differential premium is generally more applicable for the removal of restrictions on leasehold properties.

development control The implementation and enforcement of planning standards by the Urban Revelopment Authority.

Development Guide Plans (DGP) These are blueprints which map out the future physical development of specific areas. For purposes of planning, Singapore is divided into 55 planning areas. A DGP is prepared for each planning area where the broad vision of the Concept Plan is translated into specific land-use proposals like land use and density. Together, the 55 DGPs form the Master Plan.

executive condominiums (ECs) These are strata-titled apartments built by the private sector and have facilities comparable to private condominiums. However, there are some restrictions attached to it in the initial years such as eligibility conditions and minimum occupation period before it can be sold.

good class bungalows These are large size detached houses with a minimum plot size of 1,400sqm. They are found in the designated bungalow zones in Singapore.

HDB flats Public housing built by the Housing & Development Board (HDB). Majority (more than 80%) of Singaporeans stay in HDB flats.

Housing & Development Board (HDB) HDB is Singapore's public housing authority. It plans and develops public housing towns that provide Singaporeans with affordable, quality homes and living environments.

Housing Developer Sale License (SL) This is the sale license issued by the Comptroller of Housing to enable developers to develop and sell residential projects before their completion. Sales can only start after obtaining the sale license and the building plan approval.

Inland Revenue Authority of Singapore (IRAS) Acts as an agent of the government and provides services in administering, assessing, collecting and enforcing payment of taxes.

integrated resort (IR) These are integrated projects comprising entertainment and convention facilities, hotels, theme attractions, cultural amenities as well as a casino component. Singapore's two IRs are expected to be completed in 2009-2010. One is located on Sentosa Island while the other is located in the Marina Bayfront.

JTC Corporation (JTC) JTC Corporation (JTC) is Singapore's principal developer and manager of public industrial estates and related facilities in Singapore. Over the past three decades, it has developed some 7,000 hectares of industrial land and four million square meters of ready-built factories for more than 7,000 local and multinational companies. Among these are specialized parks and facilities for high-technology and biomedical industries.

Land Titles (Strata) Act This Act governs all buildings which are strata-titled. Amongst the requirements set out in the Act include the compulsory setting up of a Management Corporation (MC), application/approval for collective sale and determination of share value.

landed houses A term used to refer to low rise dwelling houses usually not more than three storeys. It includes terrace, semi-detached bungalows/ houses and bungalows/detached houses.

litho sheet A map published by the Survey Department from which plot dimensions can be ascertained.

lot number Number identifying a property for legal purposes.

management corporation or MCST A body corporate established under the Land Titles (Strata) Act which consists of all the owners of the units in a strata-titled development. The Management Corporation owns, controls and manages the common property.

Master Plan The master plan translates the broad strategies proposed in the Concept Plan into detailed plans to guide the physical development of Singapore over the next 10 to 15 years. From the Master Plan, owners, architects, planners and developers know what can be built, where and how high the buildings can be, and how intensively the land can be used. The Master Plan is reviewed every five years with the latest coming in 2003. The set of 55 Development Guide Plans (DGPs) form the master plan for Singapore.

non-landed properties This refers to condominiums and apartment housing.

planning region Singapore is divided into five planning regions to facilitate the planning of the use and development of land for the whole of Singapore. The five regions are Central Region, East Region, North East Region, North Region and West Region.

property tenure The time period (usually in years) over which the owner of the property or land enjoys the legal right of use subject to other restrictive covenants that may or may not be in place. Most properties are either freehold, 999-year or 99-year in tenure.

provisional permission (PP) This refers to the conditional approval granted by the Minister for National Development or the Competent Authority to develop any land subject to conditions in accordance with the development rules in force.

Real Estate Developers Association of Singapore (REDAS) REDAS comprises of members from all key property developers/players of Singapore and is active in making representations to all bodies, public or semi-public in nature, that concern the planning, organization, promotion, development, financing and administration of real estate development.

resale flat (HDB) A Housing & Development Board (HDB) flat available on the open resale market as opposed to direct first time flat purchases from HDB.

resale levy (HDB) This is the sum of money that a seller needs to pay if he intends to buy.

reserve list (government land sales program) A Government Land Sales site in the Reserve List will only be offered for sale via a land tender bid process if there is at least one successful application from an interested developer who is able to offer a minimum land price for the site in question that is acceptable to the government. This Government Reserve Price is usually determined by the Chief Assessor of Singapore. The successful applicant must undertake to subsequently submit a bid for the land in the tender at or above the minimum price offered by him in the application.

semi-detached house/bungalow A type of landed housing where by it comprises one half of a low rise detached building, usually not more than three storeys. The minimum plot size is 200 sq. m. and the minimum frontage is 8 m.

shophouse A low-rise building, usually less than four storeys, within a row of low rise building whereby the ground floor is used for retail use and the upper floor is used for dwelling or commercial purposes.

Singapore Institute of Surveyors and Valuers (SISV) SISV is the professional body representing the land surveyors, quantity surveyors, valuers, property managers, property consultants and real estate agents. Membership is divided into students, probationers, Member, Fellow and Honorary Fellow. To become a member, one must possess the relevant academic qualification that is recognized by the Institute, appropriate practical experience and passing the Assessment of Professional Competence.

Singapore Land Authority (SLA) The main focus of SLA is on land resource optimization, and it is responsible for the management of State land and buildings, land sales, leases, acquisitions and allocation, developing and marketing land-related information and maintaining the national land information database.

small office home office (SOHO) SOHO are generally home offices where the occupants works and resides within the same place. SOHOs are also smart homes which provide occupants with the relevant communication and technological facilities to effectively run a business.

standard factory A ready-built low rise (usually not more than 2-storeys) factory building within an industrial estate that accommodates a wide range of light to medium industries that are non-pollutive and requiring heavy floor loading and large areas of ground floor space.

Temporary Occupation Permit (TOP) The issue of TOP usually marks the building's physical completion as fit to stay. Only then can owners or tenants begin to occupy the premises. TOP is issued before CSC which denotes both legal completion and compliance with regulations.

terrace houses A type of landed housing where by several low rise houses, usually not more than three storeys, are linked together and they share common party walls. The minimum plot size is 150 sq. m. for the intermediate units and 200 sq. m. for the corner units. The minimum frontage of the buildings are 6 m. and 8 m. respectively.

townhouse A residential building designed as a single dwelling house unit with ground contact and forming part of a row of not less than three residential units with common ownership of land.

Urban Redevelopment Authority (URA) The Urban Redevelopment Authority (URA) is Singapore's national land use planning authority. URA prepares long term strategic plans, as well as detailed local area plans, for physical development, and then co-ordinates and guides efforts to bring these plans to reality.

Written Permission (WP) The approval granted by the Minister for National Development or the competent authority to develop any land subject to conditions in accordance with the development rules in force.

TWN – Taiwan

chia (甲) It is a traditional measurement unit of area used in Taiwan. Its use is limited to real estate. 1 chia = 0.96992 hectare = 2.3968 acre.

current assessed land value (公告現值) A land value used by municipalities to compute land value increment tax; it is assessed once every year by municipalities. The value is close to the market value.

dian (典權) The right to use a real property of another person and to collect profits therefrom by paying the price for the dian and taking possession of the real property for a period of not exceeding 30 years.

government announced land value (公告地價) A land value used by municipalities to compute land value tax; it is assessed once every three years by municipalities. The value is much lower than the market value.

house tax (房屋稅) A building tax is levied based on the current value of standard price and applicable tax rate, not based on the building cost or market value. It is calculated by the following formula: Standard House Price x Size (acreage) x (1 - an Applicable Depreciation Rate x the Years of Depreciation) x an Adjustment Rate based on the Level / Class of Street or Road x an Applicable Tax Rate = Payable House Tax.

land register sheet (土地登記簿) A title deed, or land ownership certificate, includes three sections, namely: description, ownership and other rights in sequence. The cover sheet is entitled with "The Land Register or Constructional Improvements of so-and-so Township/City, District, Volume number so-and-so". Each sheet inside the register shall be affixed with the seal of land registration.

land registration (土地登記) Registration of the ownership of, and other rights over, land and constructional improvements thereon. In Taiwan, land registration is carried out by the competent Special Municipality/County/ City Land Office; or it is carried out by a land registry set up ad hoc in a Special Municipality/County/City by the said Land Office.

land value increment tax (土地增值稅) A property tax is levied on the basis of the net increment of the value of land, when the ownership thereof is transferred, or after the lapse of 10 full years though the ownership thereof has not been transferred. The period of 10 full years begins from the date when the value of land is assessed for the first time. Since land value increment tax is levied on realized gains from land transactions, it is sometimes imprecisely characterized as a "capital gains" tax. The formula to calculate the net increment is: Land Value Increment = Declared Present Value at the Transfer - Original Decreed Value or the Assessed Value at the Last Transfer x Consumer Price Index Adjustment - Land Improvement Costs + Construction Benefits Fee Paid + Fee Paid for Land Consolidation.

land value tax（土地價税） A property tax is levied once every year on the basis of the government announced land value. In terms of its computation, where the total value of all lands owned by any landowner does not exceed the initial point of land value subject to progressive rates, the land value tax is levied according to the basic rate of 1.5% of the government announced land value. Where the total value of all lands owned by any landowner exceeds the initial point of land value subject to progressive rates, the land value tax on that part of the total value which exceeds the said initial point is levied at different rates.

mow（公畝） It is a traditional measurement unit of area used in Taiwan. Its use is limited to real estate. 1 mow = 0.06667 hectare = 0.16473 acre.

ping（坪） It is a traditional measurement unit of area used in Taiwan. Its use is limited to real estate. 1 ping = 3.305 square meters = 36 square feet.

sanheyuan（三合院） It is a traditional Chinese residential property, so-called a "three-side enclosed courtyard", formed with inward-facing houses on three sides.

servitudes（地役權） Servitude is the right to use the land of another person for the convenience of one's own land. The owner of the dominant land is entitled to perform such acts as are necessary for exercising or preserving his rights, provided that he shall choose the place and the method which will cause the least injury to the servient land. Furthermore, the owner of a dominant land, who makes constructions for the purpose of exercising his rights, is bound to maintain such constructions. The owner of the servient land may use the constructions as specified previously, except when it will obstruct the exercise of the servitude. In the case specified previously, the owner of the servient land shall bear his share of the expenses for the maintenance of the constructions in proportion to the interests he benefits therefrom.

siheyuan（四合院） It is a traditional Chinese residential property, or quadrangle, so-called a "four-side enclosed courtyard", formed with inward-facing houses on four sides, enclosed by walls. Such a residence offers space, comfort, and privacy. A small or medium-sized siheyuan usually has its main or only entrance gate built at the southeastern corner of the quadrangle with a screen wall just inside to prevent outsiders from peeping in.

superficies (地上權) Superficies is the right to use the land of another person with the object of owning a building or other works or bamboos or trees thereon.

THA – Thailand

ar-karn Building.

ar-karn-chud (condominium) Strata-title building.

ar-karn-soong High-rise building with a height of 23 meters or more.

ar-karn-yai-pi-ses Extra large buildings that have gross floor area of 10,000 sq. m. or more.

ar-sang-ha-rim-ma-sup Real estate.

bai-anu-yard-chai-arkarn Building permit.

bai-anu-yard-kor-sang Construction permit.

far Plot ratio or the building to land ratio.

kar-nar-din Ground lease premium.

karn-chao-choung Sub-lease.

karn-oan-sitti-karn-chao Assignment.

kong-thun-ruam-asang-ha-rim-ma-sup Real estate investment trust.

pa-si-bum-rung-thong-thi Local development tax. This tax only applies to land. The tax rate varies greatly, depending on the location and assessed value of the land. Typically, it ranges from baht 0.5 to baht 400 per rai (1,600 sq. m) (2005).

pa-si-mul-la-ka-perm Value-added tax (VAT), which is a consumption tax based on the value of goods and services offered by traders, businesses or persons in Thailand. It is calculated from the price of the goods and services. The standard rate is 7% (2005).

pa-si-rong-ruen House and land tax. This is a tax on assessed rental income and only applies to properties that are rented out. Rental contracts are typically split into three components that are taxed separately as follows: 1) rental: subject to a house and land tax of 12.5% of annual rental receipts; 2) lease of furniture: subject to a 7% VAT; and 3) service charge: subject to a 7% VAT (2005).

phang-muang Town plan.

ra-ka-pra-mern-raj-ja-karn Official assessed value.

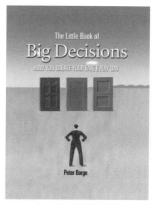

0-470-822-120

Little Book of Big Decisions contains a world of wisdom on how to make quality decisions that drive your life in the direction you want to go. Written by Peter Barge who is also the Asia Pacific Chief Executive Officer of Jones Lang LaSalle, a leading commercial real estate services firm, he shares his philosophy on how he has been able to marry the softer life skills one needs to achieve balance with the harder business skills demanded today of a global company. An active follower of Deepak Chopra, a qualified pharmaculturalist and an avid reader, Peter attributes his rich and successful life to taking time to meditate daily and honing his decision-making skills over the years.